Praise for *YES! Energy*

"Yes! Energy helps people tap into what is innately available to us—the productive, positive energy that propels us to a life of purpose and enjoyment. Loral by no means has given up on the human spirit and possibilities. Instead, she has chosen to deliver perspective and tools precisely at the time when most needed! Readers will benefit from this compelling book."

— **Stedman Graham**, best-selling author
and CEO of S. Graham & Associates

"Yes! Energy is truly inspiring. This book will help you employ all of your skills to succeed. It teaches you how to live in a world where Yes! is the winning answer. Loral Langemeier does it again with another highly recommended book."

— **Joseph Grenny**, best-selling author
and co-founder of VitalSmarts

"If you want the blueprint for obliterating the uncertainty and frustration in your life, and replacing it with incredible confidence and unbounded success, then you need to read Loral's book Yes! Energy. You already have the tools you need; Loral shows you how to use them."

— **Tom Mower, Sr.**, president and
co-founder of Sisel International

"Yes! Energy will replace the 'no energy' we were programmed with as infants. It's the no energy that keeps 97 percent of our population stuck in life. Loral has made a huge breakthrough here . . . and you will, too, by doing exactly as Loral directs you to do. I love it. This is a powerful concept that will set you free . . . Yes! It will."

— **Bob Proctor**, best-selling author

$$\{\Delta C+[f(2C)*D]+G+T\}S = \infty EOE\infty$$

YES!
Energy

ALSO BY LORAL LANGEMEIER

*The Millionaire Maker: Act, Think, and
Make Money the Way the Wealthy Do*

The Millionaire Maker's Guide to Creating a Cash Machine for Life

The Millionaire Maker's Guide to Wealth Cycle Investing

Put More Cash in Your Pocket: Turn What You Know into Dough

Please visit:

Hay House USA: **www.hayhouse.com**®
Hay House Australia: **www.hayhouse.com.au**
Hay House UK: **www.hayhouse.co.uk**
Hay House South Africa: **www.hayhouse.co.za**
Hay House India: **www.hayhouse.co.in**

YES!
Energy

The Equation to Do Less, Make More

Loral Langemeier

HAY HOUSE, INC.

Carlsbad, California • New York City
London • Sydney • Johannesburg
Vancouver • Hong Kong • New Delhi

Published and distributed in the United States by: Hay House, Inc.: www
.hayhouse.com • *Published and distributed in Australia by:* Hay House Australia
Pty. Ltd.: www.hayhouse.com.au • *Published and distributed in the United Kingdom by:* Hay House UK, Ltd.: www.hayhouse.co.uk • *Published and distributed
in the Republic of South Africa by:* Hay House SA (Pty), Ltd.: www.hayhouse.co.za
• *Distributed in Canada by:* Raincoast: www.raincoast.com • *Published in India
by:* Hay House Publishers India: www.hayhouse.co.in

Cover design: Christy Salinas • *Interior design:* Tricia Breidenthal

Library of Congress Cataloging-in-Publication Data

Langemeier, Loral.
  Yes! energy : the equation to do less, make more / Loral Langemeier.
    p. cm.
  ISBN 978-1-4019-3647-1 (hardback) -- ISBN 978-1-4019-3648-8 (tradepaper) 1.
Self-actualization (Psychology) I. Title.
  BF637.S4.L337 2012
  650.1--dc23
                              2011041289

Hardcover ISBN: 978-1-4019-3647-1
Tradepaper ISBN: 978-1-4019-3648-8
Digital ISBN: 978-1-4019-3649-5

15 14 13 12   4 3 2 1
1st edition, February 2012

Printed in the United States of America

*This book is dedicated to my team and
the Live Out Loud Community, those I am
here to serve. Together we create Yes! Energy.*

CONTENTS

LETTER
FROM LORAL

Ever notice there are some people who just have *that thing?* My old best friend, Diane, and I used to call it the gift. "He's got the gift," she'd observe. These people are certain; they are sure; and they move forward with an easy, graceful energy and optimism. It's empowering, timeless, and endless, and if you're fortunate enough to catch it, it's contagious.

Well, you too can be one of those people. You can capture *that thing*—because you already have it. It's within you. It's just a little atrophied muscle that needs to be rebuilt. Once you rediscover it, you can live an unlimited life of abundance, extreme optimism, and energy.

But what exactly *is* it?

This gift, *that thing,* is Yes! Energy. I've discovered a formula, a nonmathematical equation that will help you make Yes! Energy a big part of your life. That's what this book is about: it's a journey through the *Energy Equation,* helping you learn each of its components so that you can have all the Yes! Energy you need to accomplish your goals, reach your dreams, and do less and make more.

I'm an educator and motivational speaker. I run a global business focused on entrepreneurship and wealth building. It's my mission to go around the world and create supportive, encouraging, abundant communities that operate as entrepreneurial microeconomies. My company, my communities, and my friends and family live by the idea that when you lead and commit to Yes! Energy, you are optimistic and solution oriented—able to do less, make more, and live the life you want.

Our mantra is: *Say yes now, then figure out how.* By "figure out how," we mean sourcing solutions from a greater power, and gathering a team of capable, supportive people who know *how to do what you don't* to get to your goals. It's a sacred sequence that begins with a greater power; is supported by community; and keeps you moving forward, toward a solution.

Too many do too much for too little. They believe that working harder is the answer, so they push and exert and get nowhere. When you grab on to extreme optimism and energy sourced from a higher power, when you have community and support, when you have Yes! Energy, you can actually do the opposite: you can *do less, make more.*

Of course, the questions are:

- *Where is it?*

- *How do I get it?*

- *What do I do?*

Yes! Energy is not a theoretical concept. It is a proven process, formulated in a sacred sequence called the *Energy Equation.* This is not a mathematical equation, nor does it follow an "order of operations," since, over time, many of these steps are taken in concert with each other. It is a memory device of symbols that are easy to follow. It is a formula that will take you from A to B, from where you are to where you want to be, fast and easy. While there will always be that age-old struggle of our time (events occurring as we hope they will) versus God time (events occurring as they actually will), this formula allows you to quickly and gracefully bridge the gap between where you are and where you can be. In three weeks, in one year, in five years, for the rest of your life, you can get from here to there with a lot less struggle (*do less*) and a lot more productivity (*make more*) than you ever imagined.

When you are aware and have knowing energy, *you know that you know.* You have direct access to the ever-present solution. Life has the answers you need. Once you know how to sequence properly—to tap into the vibration that comes from a greater power and hear what it has to say to you, personally and directly—you can move forward, leading your life with optimism, certainty, and passion.

Fun, right? Ha! And we've only begun. When you really get it, you'll really know, and you will stand up and cheer for the simplicity of it all.

The *Energy Equation* will help you at home, in business, and in every area of your life. You will find—no matter what you're doing, no matter the issue or the goal—that you can tap into your Yes! Energy to *do less, make more.* Do less work, do less of what you're not good at doing, do less wasting time, do less worrying, do less "bad" in your life. Now you can make more money, make more time, make more happiness, and make more good and love in your world.

I've always had a Spirit-sourced solution orientation, and that's fed my extreme optimism and energy. When I have a problem, I use this formula to source God, find team support, and sequence toward a solution. Although I've taken a few big knocks, which I'll elaborate on in these pages, eventually I've gotten back into forward motion by using my Yes! Energy. Even during the worst of times, when I was at my lowest—being told no, pushed down by negative energy and people—I was solution oriented. I got into the *Energy Equation* and soon enough, I was back in the saddle, riding certainty and optimism.

$$\infty$$

In the fall of 2009, I was in a private master-mind group—a think tank—with leaders in my industry. Among the group was Reid Tracy, president and CEO of the publisher Hay House. We sat next to each other, and he acknowledged the great work I was doing with my clients and in my community. He shared with me how amazing Hay House is, with its engaging events, radio and Internet presence, and author-reader interaction.

Not one to hold back on my intention, I quickly stated, "I want to be a Hay House author." Although my previous books were on the finance shelf, Reid nodded his encouragement and told me that the day I wanted to share my personal story and write the behind-the-scenes account of a woman who runs a multimillion-dollar global enterprise, he'd publish it.

At this time, the recession was gathering its painful momentum and hitting people hard. Yet my company and I kept moving forward strong. As time went on, I noticed that more and more people were asking me how we were having such success, despite the numerous obstacles. So, a year after we met, Reid and I finally decided it was time I shared the story.

This is a very personal book for me. Inspired by others who have hit rock bottom and found their way up and out of bad situations, I decided to write a book in which I share the good, the bad, and the ugly. The ugly has been *ugly*, those times when I compromised my values and who I am, and let bad, dark energy into my life. Yet, fortunately, I surfaced up and out of that muck into empowerment. In these pages, I reveal the tools I've used to motivate myself past the obstacles and difficulty into Yes! Energy.

If you've gone down the wrong path, lost yourself, and compromised your values, and you're looking to find your soul again, you need to tap into the sacred sequence and source a solution. If this economy has been brutal to you and you feel physically, emotionally, or spiritually wounded, you need to engage the *Energy Equation*. If you are making it, but it takes every inch of everything you've got and you know your life can have more ease, grace, and clarity, then you need to find your Yes! Energy.

After you read this book, please go to **http://www.liveoutloud .com**, and tell me what you think. I'd like to hear how you rediscovered the power within you to live and lead in extreme optimism and energy. I want to hear your stories, your journey. The answer to the life you always wanted—to do less, make more—is in the equation of Yes! Energy. Go get it.

— **Loral Langemeier**
Lake Tahoe, Nevada

INTRODUCTION

At a trust- and estate-planning event of several hundred people, average age 70, I was asked why I was out beating my particular, to some *peculiar,* drum so loudly. The drum, if you don't know, is that:

- We live in a time of being busy, but not productive.

- Too many are doing too much for too little benefit.

- Much potential talent is going undiscovered and underutilized.

- It's time again to dream—to innovate, create, and expand—and generate ease, grace, and clarity.

This particular group of folks remembered a simpler time. They recalled when the input of effort had a direct, clear output. They viewed ability and accountability as admirable traits. They longed for that era when entrepreneurs made economies. They also knew that they could, back in those days, create enough time and make more than enough money to enjoy family, friends, a good living, and great moments.

All that is available again to us now. That's why I'm out beating my drum.

Too many people are having the wrong conversation, and we are suffering because of it. There's frustration and fear when there should be hope and excitement. What's needed is an easy shift, a twist of awareness and action, that can spiral these cycles up into abundance and fulfillment.

The hurtful messages out there are about tucking in, and since it requires no skill or energy to get small, it's selling well to an audience who would like to do nothing or be nothing.

That's not you if you picked up this book. If you picked up this book, you know you have, and want to nurture, the Yes! Energy to do less, make more. You're not alone. A lot of people want more out of life. They want their lattes, they want fun toys, they want to feel good, and they want to work less and engage in life more. Hooray for them. I'm beating the drum for them, for *you*, to say "Yes!" instead of "no."

You have a choice in this lifetime to be afraid and crouch low or to live an expansive life of *Yes!* where dreams come true. You can choose to dream and create.

You have a choice to direct energy into denial and losing or into action and building, creating, expanding, and generating. You can choose to act and build.

You have a choice to deny your inherent gifts or to affirm and use your skills—your enormous, untapped gifts—to generate wealth and expand opportunities. You can choose to use your gifts and have abundance.

You have a choice to play defense or go on offense, to follow or to lead. You can choose to win, to lead, to have a vision that sees opportunities.

By Not Taking Risks, We Risk It All

I asked a colleague and fellow author in the finance-education field why he teaches saving and debt planning, rather than wealth building and abundance. "You know that's the right way," I said.

"I do know it, Loral," he acknowledged. "But it doesn't sell. People won't do it. You set them up to fail by trying. They like to play small. People can't handle more than that. They like to go easy."

"But easy is harder in the end."

"Most people don't look that far ahead," he replied. "That's why I'm selling the concept of what they can do now."

"I'm selling what they can do now, too," I said. "I just have more confidence in people's ability to commit to and lead their lives."

"Ha!" he scoffed. "That's what the wealthy and educated do."

"Exactly," I said. "And everyone can do it. This isn't a new conversation; it's what the wealthy have always known."

"Why doesn't everyone do it, then?"

"Because no one is telling them how," I replied. "They don't even hear about it. They don't know it's an option. It's been kept quiet, hush-hush, for the few."

"I'm just selling books people can read and put on the bed stand, Loral," he said. "You know, empty calories. Even if you can get people motivated, they won't do it."

"Well, I believe in the human spirit too much," I said.

He gave me a pat on the back and walked away.

I shared this dialogue with the room of several hundred older folks.

"How did we get so unresourceful?" one of them asked.

"My kids have more difficult lives than we ever did," another said. "Their schedules are filled; they hardly see their spouses; they work incredibly hard, or seem to, and can never catch up financially."

Another stood up. "That's the problem. I made a good living, built up a company, and I'd consider myself wealthy. But my kids are financially illiterate. If I gave them the business, it would tank. I know it's my fault—I should have taught them how to generate the wealth we had, but they didn't seem interested."

"And they're smart, right?" I said. "And able?"

"Very," he replied with a sigh. "But we live in a time when everyone wants a safe job, a pension, a retirement account, social security, and someone else to take the risks."

"By *not* taking risks, by not living our full potential, *we risk it all*," I said.

The room cheered. They were from another time. A time of going for it, a time of "Who better than us?"

They knew. One of them stood up to say so: "Thanks for reminding me, Loral."

∞

The United States of America and other countries like it are prosperous. But people are not necessarily energetic, positive, or living well. That's where we have yet another choice. We can sink into a lazy mind-set and shrink our vision and goals or rise to the challenge and make the great countries even greater.

As for the country in which I live, the U.S., we're living during the best time to generate and build wealth. Statistically, more people from other countries are buying up land in Arizona than Americans are. It's a fire sale out there, and we're letting others take our assets from us. Yet too many Americans have chosen this time, the period after recession and depression when dollars are most powerful and opportunity greatest, to save, get small, lick their wounds, and say, "No, not right now."

That's why I beat the drum so loudly. I'm pushing a message that can work side by side with the "Manage risk, be responsible" message, but this one offers so much more. This message is about having extreme optimism to stay positive despite frustrations, and a great energy that will let you accomplish anything you want. It's about saying "Yes!" right now to the *Energy Equation.*

Extreme Optimism and Energy—the ∞EOE∞

When you hit a hurdle or have a problem, you need to recognize the problem and realize that it's being delivered to you as a sign to pay attention. The obstacle is shouting out that you're immersed in the wrong solution. You need to take the hit, look to a greater power for a better answer, and realize that there *is* a better answer and that you can, in fact, be okay. Then you leverage that energy by turning to others to help, and source your team.

A great team is vital to a positive, calm, clear approach to life. By "team," I mean surrounding yourself with the right people—those who will feed your energy and optimism. I'm able to do so much in my life and expand my world because I have teams of people who are much better at doing certain things than I am. I don't waste my time trying to do things that I don't do well. There's no way I'm going to spend hours working on a website or doing my own accounting when I can spend that same time playing with my kids. With the right team, there's no need to.

When I'm working hard, I'm doing it wrong. Most of the time, my team can execute much better than I can, since I am not as skilled as they are. When I'm in the way, it's hard, slow, and I'm doing too much. When I'm in the *Energy Equation,* I realize I can say "Yes!" now, and figure out how by getting other people to do what I don't know how to do anyway. Usually, when I'm out of sync, I'm probably not the one to be doing the work, so instead I get a team so I can do less, make more. Everyone wins.

The times in my life that I was compromised were when I let others in whom I shouldn't have. When those individuals aren't in my life, things are cleaner and calmer again.

It's that simple and direct. If others in your life are aligned to the spiritual energy with which you resonate, then you're in a different place. This is the Law of Vibration. My friend and mentor Bob Proctor puts it very well; he says this vibration "accounts for the difference between mind and matter, between the physical and the nonphysical worlds." As I like to say, *it's that thing in between.* That thing that can't be seen, but it can be felt, and it pulls and plays at all of our interactions. If the team is working together in the right vibration, then all is in sync.

Let's be clear. The strongest energy always wins. That's it, no contest. No matter what the situation, who the players, where the location, *whoever is in control of the energy is in control of the room.* Strong doesn't mean loud, manic, dominating, or controlling. Strong means certain, clear, motivated, and serving. Better energy is the answer to a more fulfilling life, to moving out of frustration and into hope—to abundance.

Determined, sure, authentic, straightforward, humble, motivated, certain, confident—that's good energy.

Optimism is knowing you can access a solution at all times. Although you may not have it right now, it's there, and it's your responsibility to be forward looking, *knowing*. If it's not there, you're looking in the wrong place. It's time to find that solution by using energy and optimism that comes from a higher power and uses the support and collaboration of a team.

That's the key to having exactly the life you want. I know. Not only have I created the life I want, but as one of the world's leading mentors of both men and women in the wealth-building space, I've helped thousands of others do it, too—and I'm not talking about starting from a place of strength.

I developed this methodology because I needed it myself. I've been knocked over more than a few times. Yet, despite the blows, I still stand, and I still deliver.

Getting Personal

As an educator in the wealth-building industry, I've shared some of my personal journey, but mostly, I've presented from a position of strength and accomplishment. Recently, however, onstage at a seminar in Australia, I was surprised to discover that when I revealed some of the more painful and frustrating parts of my life, the energy in the room hummed at a higher level. And so, I shared a bit more, this time about some particularly offensive attacks I had endured. The audience members were silent, on the edge of their seats, hanging on every word.

I stopped. "Ah, what's going on?"

One of the younger men, on a short leave from the military, stood up. "Loral, I've heard you speak a few times now, and I must say that my impression was that you had it fairly easy. Now I'm hearing you made it through some stormy patches, and I find it quite encouraging."

"Encouraging?"

"Yes," he said. "I know I can make it, too."

That's when I realized I had a whole other story to tell. A story about energy, commitment, certainty, faith, and leadership. Previous books I've written under *The Millionaire Maker* series were business titles that emphasized leadership. This book has a similar focus. Those who understand the true meaning of leadership understand how to propel their lives into extreme optimism and energy. *I believe that if we lead our own lives, we can create the lives we want.* Lives in Yes! Energy.

Recent economic events threw a lot of people, including me. It's not been easy. But there is a way out and up. I came out of the rocky markets, and I'm pushing through this recession with some losses, but more wins. On this tumultuous road I turned over some heavy obstacles and excavated several insights.

One of these was:

The *Energy Equation*

$$\{\Delta C+ [F(2C)^*D]+G+T\}S = \infty EOE\infty$$

As I mentioned in my letter at the start of this book, this equation requires no math. I'm using letters and symbols as a memory device. The name of the equation itself, $\infty EOE\infty$, has the infinity signs flanking the initials for *extreme optimism* and *energy* to imply that the formula can provide endless doses of both.

As you'll see below and in the parts of the book covering the formula and its components, the letters and symbols stand for each aspect of the *Energy Equation*. For example, I used the Greek letter delta, Δ, for "change," followed by the letter C, for "conversation," to indicate changing the conversation as a first step.

There are eight vital factors that make up the *Energy Equation*. They are covered in the five parts of the book as follows:

Part I: An overall look at the *Energy Equation* itself, the $\infty EOE\infty$

Part II: (1) A willingness to *change the conversation*, ΔC

Part III: (2) Sourcing a higher power, and the commitment
            of *faith*, F

            (3) *Certainty* and
            (4) *Confidence*, 2C
            (5) A renewed focus on *dreams*, D

Part IV: (6) A pledge to share inherent *gifts*, G

Part V: (7) A supportive, positive, motivating *team*, T
            (8) Proper *sequencing*, the distinct technique of
            doing the right thing at the right time, S

With this equation, you can achieve the ultimate, extreme levels of continuous energy that will propel you through your day. You've seen people like this. They seem to be able to get thousands of things done. They're happy, fun, and optimistic. You think they may be unreal or too good to be true. But the fact is, this state of energy, of living, is very attainable. With the *Energy Equation,* you can do it, too.

Throughout the five parts of this book, I explain all of the components of the *Energy Equation.* I chose to divide it this way so I could cover each component in as in-depth a fashion as possible. Although everything in the equation can occur almost simultaneously and each factor works in concert with the others, I present them in this sequence so as to build the formula as logically as possible. You'll find, though, that *all* of the factors pop up in each section.

The five parts of the book are laid out as follows:

— In the **first** part of the book, I introduce the idea of Yes! Energy by sharing, as I do throughout the book, a few examples of how I used the *Energy Equation* to overcome some of the obstacles in my life. When I decided to write about my recent experiences and discoveries, I asked several of my colleagues and affiliates what it was they wanted to know about my process and methodology. A lot of their curiosity surrounded my psychology, how I got up again after being knocked down, and how I kept negative thoughts from suggesting I quit and give up. They also asked a lot about my ability to integrate my business and personal lives, as well as stay motivated and keep my energy up. That's why, as I mentioned before, I decided to write this book with Hay House. I wanted to share my personal experiences, so I do throughout. In this first section, I also provide an overview of the *Energy Equation* formula.

— The **second** part is devoted solely to the first component of the formula, *changing the conversation*, ΔC. This factor requires an entire section, since shifting one's perceptions and attitude about, and engagement with, life is the very foundation of Yes! Energy.

— The **third** part of the book covers *faith, certainty, confidence,* and *dreams,* $[F(2C)*D]$, all of which, as indicated by the parentheses and brackets in which they sit, connect organically in the formula.

— The **fourth** part of the book focuses solely on *gifts,* G. Yes! Energy is fueled by our own gifts, and we must uncover the many talents and blessings we have and put them to good use. This topic merits a full section because although gifts can be fuel for the fire, they are, too often, doused. So this part identifies, so as to change, the ways in which we overlook—and, worse, sabotage—our best assets.

— The **fifth** part of the book covers two of the most dynamic and overarching factors of the formula—*team* and *sequencing,* $\{+ T\}S$—as well as a summary explanation of how the *Energy Equation* can help anyone do less, make more. Although presented last, team and sequencing are anything but least. As I mentioned, all parts of the equation are occurring at all times, almost simultaneously, and team and sequencing are really like the wheels of a car. They sit beneath, and support and steer, everything that your Yes! Energy vehicle can do.

Finally, I sum up the book as I do all my finance books, with a look at legacy. We consider how you can pass the gift of Yes! Energy on to young adults and children, whether your own or those with whom you interact in your life.

Regardless of your current situation and eventual goals, I know that change is not easy. You may want support. As I referenced earlier, I have a website (**http://www.liveoutloud.com**) you can join for free, and communities around the world devoted to the ideas in this book. These communities are great place to connect and begin to find your team. You are not in this alone. Nor should you be. There is as little or as much encouragement available to you as you need.

I am very grateful for this opportunity to share my stories, as well as my insights and discoveries. And I look forward to your thoughts. I hope to engage you in a new conversation as you step into extreme optimism and energy. Start reading today, the sooner the better, because a week, a month, and then a year from now, you'll be amazed by how much better every area of your life can continue to be when you're in your Yes! Energy.

THE
ENERGY
EQUATION

$$\{\Delta C + [F(2C) * D] + G + T\}S = \infty EOE\infty$$

"There are no rules
here, we're trying to
accomplish something."

— ENTRY SIGN TO INVENTOR
THOMAS EDISON'S LAB

THE OBSTACLE COURSE

Energy's Promise and the Speed of Attitude

How do you capture extreme optimism and energy? That's the discovery I made over the past few years of going through my own trials and tribulations: how to generate endless, exciting, life-engaging, positive Yes! Energy that flows from you to others and from them back to you again. It's a life force that's vital, dramatic, and thrilling.

And you have it. You have access to it *right now*. Once you know how to use it, you'll never stop. You will know how to access it always.

The first place from which this life force comes is a core vibration of certainty and optimism. This core vibration, in turn, comes from a greater power. It's a calm, collected energy. That's *the thing,* the gift I mentioned on the first page of this book. It's also so much more. Whenever I'm in a tight spot where things don't feel right—when I'm not being the best Loral I know I can be—I take full responsibility. I look to God, and I ask for clarity and understanding. Then I look to myself and I say, "Pay attention, Loral. What's going on here?"

Because I choose to live an inspired life, one sourced from Spirit, I know that there is a plan for me and everyone and everything. This gives me optimism and certainty. And because I'm anchored in solution, because I know there is a way forward, I then take the optimism and certainty delivered from Spirit, and I turn to my team and do just that: I move forward. Next thing I know, I'm in my Yes! Energy. My energy is conserved, yet I'm moving full steam ahead. I'm calm, I'm at ease, I'm hopeful. Neither negativity nor failure has a chance when I'm truly in this state, when I'm in the flow, sourcing energy and optimism.

Unfortunately, I do not do this all of the time. In fact, recently, I did not do it at all. I was in a situation where I moved away from living the core vibration; I was outside my own energy, losing myself, compromising my values, attracting dark, bad energy. It was awful. Then, because (a) I went back to Spirit, (b) got the help of my team, and (c) remembered how to source my extreme optimism and energy, I found my soul again. Fortunately, I'm back in good times after a terrible interlude.

I'm sure you've had your fair share of obstacles. My goal here is to reveal an idea that will push you up and above and beyond those frustrations into a life of true freedom.

I did it. I grew up working on a farm, started my own businesses, worked my way through school, pushed my way into a dog-eat-dog field, built a brand and a global enterprise . . . and then saw bits and pieces come crumbling down around me. After several ounces of introspection and a pound of action, I picked myself up, dusted myself off, and rebuilt everything into a life that's even better than before.

And so I know you can do it, too.

How? Well, it's a little bit of strategy, with a whole lot of support, but the most important factor of all is energy management.

"I am so sick of people talking about time management, Loral," said a woman at one of my seminars in Calgary, Canada. "I can't stand it if one more person says that I need to find a way to better balance my schedule."

"You're right," I said. "It's not time management; it's *energy management.*"

The others nodded. The room was in full agreement.

People can talk all they want about time management, but as anyone who's ever tried to fit 25 hours of life into a 24-hour day knows, that's a misguided pursuit. Too many of us have treaded on an endless loop of "not enough time." Time management is not the answer. The solution is something else altogether.

It's energy management. The source of energy, the fuel to be managed, comes from, as Bob Proctor and the Beach Boys knew, good vibrations. These good vibrations come from the surf and from something higher and greater. Wayne Dyer, in his book *Inspiration: Your Ultimate Calling,* put it so well:

> The reason I feel inspired isn't because the world looks perfect. Rather, it's the other way around: The reason the world looks perfect to me is because I'm in-Spirit—a person who chooses to live an inspired life. I'm able to stay in a state of gratitude from the moment I awake early in the morning right up until I close my eyes while falling asleep; and throughout each day, I'm reminded that staying in-Spirit is really about staying in vibrational harmony.

Yay. I love that. Vibrational harmony.

The *Energy Equation* works. I know, because it has saved me on a number of occasions. The following are three stories from the roller coaster.

1. The Stork Surprises Me

In the late '90s, I was just starting my business, trying to make my way into what was clearly a male-dominated industry. After some time in the wealth-education arena, learning different models and business strategies, I found my way to a speaking circuit of educators and motivational leaders. These stages attracted people interested in finance, investing, and personal success in every category imaginable.

I had some products to sell in the form of instructional CDs and workbooks, and the stages were the perfect platform for my energy and message. I soon discovered that whether it was a room of 10 or 200, I could get people excited and engaged in a distinct, compelling, and inspiring conversation. I liked the stages . . . a lot. But then my message and products started to sell better than those of the other speakers. I soon sensed a competitive edginess directed toward me.

Although I'm ambitious in my pursuits, I prefer collaboration to competition. This new vibe made me uncomfortable, so I sourced my Yes! Energy, engaged the *Energy Equation,* and worked hard to inspire my colleagues to partner up. My theme was authenticity and mutual respect. My efforts were rewarded, and soon enough, I had some great friends and associates in the field.

In 1999, just as I was getting into my groove again and really building my business, I found out I was pregnant. I was also single. There was a steady stream of advice from a lot of people, most of it unsolicited. But the most disappointing lecture came from one of my mentors. He pulled me aside at an event and asked me my plans. He knew that I had a goal to make a million dollars by the age of 35, and I was 33 at the time.

"I'm accelerating my plan to make a million dollars. I want to make it before this baby's born."

"There's no way," he said.

"There's no way what?"

"There's no way you can be a single mother and be successful," he said firmly. "Do not have this baby. A baby is a liability."

The memory of those hateful words is still vivid. An ugly feeling passed between us, and I stepped back as his intent sunk in. From my view, though, the situation was the situation. I was *not* going to change my goal, and I *was* going to have my baby. Fortunately, the obstacles brought me face-to-face with the solution, the key to moving forward, sourcing the core vibration through the sacred sequence.

Which then left me with only one question: *So what—now what?*

I did exactly what I said I would do. I accelerated my goal, all through real-estate buying and selling, and made my first million just before my 34th birthday. Three months later I had a beautiful baby boy.

Then it got difficult again. I'd planned to take six weeks off and had my nanny set up so that after that I could go, go, go. But then the nanny fell through. My bookkeeper, my assistant, and I scrambled. We all pitched in, me nursing every two hours, while my team—these two great women who at first were just employees and who were now so much more to me—surrounded my son and me in our home office, pressing forward with our budding business.

As every mother of a newborn knows, I had moments when I wanted to fall apart and just cry. But I didn't. I couldn't. I was building a business, and my son was counting on me. Although I was looking for immediate solutions, I had to be patient. I knew I couldn't create chaos by running around crazy creating the wrong solutions.

I had my team, and I kept sourcing Spirit. I knew there was a solution if I tapped the *Energy Equation.* That's when a couple showed up next door. Their twin sons were grown, and they loved the idea of spending time with my son, taking over the duties of the nanny who had fallen through. They are now two of the most important people in my life.

2. The Downfall of a Database

Sometimes, it feels like life is throwing one curveball after another. There are good times, no doubt; and for the fortunate, and those with the right perspective, the good outweighs the bad. But even so, when the hits come, they hurt. Bad. Especially when you are sensitive, which, like most humans, I am. Although I perceive my sensitivity as a strength, as a gift, it makes me, like everyone, vulnerable.

I remember early on in building my current business when I felt as if the company had been delivered a fatal blow. I'd always heard that the person with the biggest database wins, so for years I'd been building up ours. This chestnut about databases is true, of course, because revenue is generated by customers, and customers are generated by marketing—so if you don't gather and organize the names, phone numbers, and e-mails of the people interested in your product or services, you will never make any money. We were always building our database. The time, energy, and effort to collect a market for our goods and services represented a substantial investment.

One morning back in 2002, following a huge snowstorm, I negotiated my way around fallen trees and trudged into our Northern California offices to discover that we'd lost our power. There'd been a power surge in the county. The lights were out; people were scrambling to reorganize their offices, shuffling paper, making cell-phone calls, everyone attempting a productive day.

One of the information-technology professionals approached me, and his face was as white as the view out our picture window. I put my hand on his shoulder, concerned he had suffered a loss. Fortunately, he hadn't. But *we* had.

He lifted his head, his eyes looking everywhere but at me. "We lost it."

"The power?"

He shook his head. "Everything."

"What everything?" I asked, still not comprehending the magnitude of what he was trying to tell me.

"Everything. The database."

It was like a straight shot to my gut. I locked in, but his expression was pure misery. I caught my breath. "Everything? I lost my whole database? My names, addresses . . ."

"Yes."

I saw four years of work flash into the ether—gone. "Wait a minute," I said, searching for clarity, waving my arms as if it would clear the fog. "We're okay, we're okay. We backed it up. Our tech team backed it up. You promised me, I asked you, you said that it was handled. We wouldn't not—"

He put a hand up. "We thought we did. But we didn't."

"Are you telling me that we have no backups? We didn't back anything up?"

He shook his head no.

We stood in the center of the office, just staring at each other. Then another employee approached. "Well, we lost it," he said.

"We know," replied the IT guy. "The database is gone."

"And the QuickBooks."

"What?" Now the room was spinning. We'd lost all of our marketing *and* accounting, in one morning. I dared not ask, but I did. "We didn't back that up either, did we?"

They didn't bother to respond. I was left thinking, *Wow, what have I done?* I couldn't imagine how I didn't back up the data or the accounting, or make sure anyone else did. To this day, I'm clear that this was one of the biggest mistakes we'd ever made.

There we were, smack-dab in the middle of a big old impediment to our forward motion. Part of me wanted to call the town and ask how in the heck in this day and age of high-tech breaker and relay switches, a surge of power could radiate to an entire county. Of course, I knew that was an unfair desire, laying blame elsewhere when I'd not protected my own system, let alone even backed up my data. Part of me wanted to just sit down and cry, if only for a second. Another part of me wanted to throw a chair.

Soon, it sunk in. The situation was the situation, and there was absolutely nothing we could do about it. Fortunately, the obstacles brought us face-to-face with the solution, the key to moving forward, the leadership I'd need to take by engaging my Yes! Energy.

Which then left us with only one question, again: *So what— now what?*

Fortunately, we'd saved paper files. We hired an army of data-entry staffers and got back to it. Diligently and persistently, our team took each piece of paper and reentered the information into the system. By hand, we recovered 60 percent of everything. Better than nothing.

And I gathered some good out of it:

— The **first** thing I did was change our process. Although we already had a daily system of data control and backup, I led from a place of confirmation and checking in, instead of just assuming.

— The **second** thing I did was create better communication with the tech team.

— The **third** was that I never again took anything for granted as far as what was being done, and when, with our systems and our technology. I realized too late, but early enough, that just because we had a tech team, it didn't mean the team was actually doing their jobs.

— Which led me to the **fourth** good thing, which was that from that point on, I instilled in my brain the need *to lead, and never blame—to inspire what I expected.* I learned to stay ahead of these issues, and I made backup and controls an early part of the sequencing of all of our systems and processes.

Although it seemed demoralizing at the time, it was actually a good time to make such a big mistake. In the decade since then, our operations have grown exponentially. If we didn't have the proper security, database backups, system protections, and storage features in place, we'd be vulnerable to losses much greater than the one we experienced in 2002.

How did we recover so quickly? We sourced the *Energy Equation.*

3. Anyone Can Sue

"You're not in business until you've been sued," a mentor said to me by way of consolation when I first got sued.

Lawsuits are horrible. They're mean, ugly, and always feel terribly unfair. Anyone in their right mind, except lawyers, doesn't like them. Unfortunately, because we live in a litigious society, where there's plenty of entitlement and not enough accountability to go around, lawsuits are pervasive.

Someone also once told me that some people consider lawsuits to be part of their wealth plan. These people actually try to put themselves in situations that will allow them to sue someone. Yikes—talk about lazy and irresponsible. That's the way it is, though, in these times. Despite the fact that we have an amazingly well-thought-out Constitution that governs our legal system, lawsuits thrive against the spirit of that important document, fed by a motto of "guilty until proven innocent."

My business is financial and entrepreneurial education, and we execute on- and offline education programs, targeting beginners to multimillionaires. We have a beautiful conference facility in a world-class destination—Lake Tahoe, Nevada—to which people who want to be wealth builders and entrepreneurs come from all over the world.

Some of my biggest obstacles came hard and fast when the economy turned sour in 2007 and 2008. During that time, many investors and entrepreneurs did poorly in their ventures. Not unusual, since the whole banking and finance system needed a bailout. Some people were looking for someone to blame, and a few of our students and clients put a big bull's-eye on my back. At one point, I received some advice to "hit the bankruptcy button" and let everything go so that there was nothing to sue. I was told that for many people, that's the way out.

But I refused. I couldn't comprehend the idea. To me that was like getting into a pickup game, discovering it's too difficult or that some people are playing unfair, calling foul, taking my ball, and going home. No way. I'll take the hits and play until it's dark out. Or at least until the whistle blows. I considered my Yes! Energy, addressed the hits, and dealt with them.

During a particularly tough economic period, I was sued by a party that accompanied the lawsuit with a nasty, ugly public-relations smear campaign. My reputation was on the line. In previous situations, our company always immediately addressed and took care of lawsuits. Our policy is to deal with each person as the situation requires and make sure our side of the street is clean. With this approach, we'd made it through the rain that poured down from the recession, and helped several others do the same. When this PR campaign and lawsuit came a few years after every single recession-related lawsuit had been resolved, it really threw us for a loop.

I believe in the power and purpose of entrepreneurship, so I play big and often in the world of private equity. Most of the great innovations of the world are due to the risks taken by great thinkers, inventors, and visionaries; and I write and talk about the appeal of this type of direct asset allocation. That, however, does not a lawsuit make. Just because I introduce two people at a bar, it doesn't mean they can blame me when they get pregnant. Which was exactly the gist of this particular lawsuit and smear campaign.

The obstacles brought us, falsely accused and disarmed, face-to-face with the solution, the key to moving forward. I sourced my energy and optimism, got my team in place, and addressed only one question: *So what—now what?*

Fortunately, a great team of lawyers and accountants brought the truth to light. We soon discovered that the party filing suit had: (1) made some missteps with quite a few people, (2) illegally gathered funds for deals, (3) gotten personally involved with a CEO to whom monies were transferred without the proper paperwork or contracts, (4) been sued in a class-action suit, and (5) lost a primary source of income and business. Finding themselves in trouble, these people decided to look for a third party to blame and a new wealth plan, so they sued me.

I've moved on. I hope they have, too. The best thing I did was engage the *Energy Equation* to preserve my optimism and protect my energy.

Before I break down the equation, let's consider, in the next chapter, a few important things about optimism and energy.

Following each chapter, there is a series called:

Inquiry—Exercise—Next Steps

The objective is to help you shift your actions, build insights, and change perspectives. Consider writing your responses in a journal so you can monitor your progress. I've also made all of the inquiries available for download on **http://www.liveoutloud.com**. You can join, blog, and share, as well as go through the "Inquiry—Exercise—Next Steps" process as many times as you want, at various stages in your life. If you ever have a question, you can ask me directly from the website. Regardless of whether you read one chapter a day or one a week, over time you will see a significant change in your life.

∞EOE∞

CHAPTER 1

The Inquiry:

Consider the past few years. What were the most difficult obstacles you had to overcome in your life (with respect to career, money, family, health, or relationships)?

The Exercise:

Focus on one of these moments. Replay it in your mind. Then consider:

1. What was it, specifically, about this situation that drained your energy most? Was it the obstacle, your attitude, your approach, or the results?

2. Consider the people with whom you were involved. Who were they? Were they helpful or hurtful?

3. What ideas/beliefs/values did you hold most dear at the time? Was that framework threatened or nurtured? Has that shifted?

Next Steps:

Write one phrase or sentence that describes your perspective on that situation then. Write a second phrase or sentence that describes your perspective on that situation now.

Are these the same?

1. If **yes,** consider if you are stuck in the story of that obstacle. What's keeping you in that problem?

2. If **no,** and you moved through it with success, to what/whom do you attribute that?

SWITCHED **ON**

Calmly Bursting Through Inertia

Energy and extreme optimism are everything. You've seen it yourself. You've perhaps been won over by someone and later thought, *Wow, what a phenomenal energy she has.* Or you've seen someone motivate a group with one terrific burst of enthusiasm, infusing each person with hope and optimism.

Great coaches, teachers, preachers, politicians . . . they all have great energy. In fact, you could put someone out in the world with great, high energy and a bad idea and pit him against someone with an amazing idea and low energy, and see who empowers the crowd toward action. Unfortunately, this has been witnessed in history with world leaders. The dictators and tyrants shared an exuberance that infused passive followers with hateful, regressive ideas; while some of the best, brightest, and most progressive minds of history were left to languish in anonymity.

I see it in my community over and over. A woman sits on the edge of her seat, leaning toward her audience confidently and calmly, and assuredly connects with those around her. Another sits with arms folded, head down, eyes passive, and can't connect with a single person. It's more than body language. It's an ability to push through stasis and inertia to elevate wavelengths, move mountains.

This push is not loud; it's not manic, frantic, or wild. Positive energy and extreme optimism are faith based, so the effect is calm, confident, and certain. Those who emanate a frenzy of hysterics are projecting a fear-based, not faith-based, energy. I've heard people declare that they are taking control, only to *act* controlling, not even aware that they're disengaging those around them. That's a reactive, anxious, almost resentful energy. As Eckhart Tolle asks in *The Power of Now,* "Do you realize that the energy you thus emanate is so harmful in its effects that you are in fact contaminating yourself as well as those around you?"

Those who commit to Yes! Energy lead their lives from a core knowing of calm, relaying a positive energy and optimism that is contagious and life affirming to those around them.

I'm fortunate in that I get to travel across the globe and educate people on entrepreneurship and financial freedom. One of my favorite places to go is Australia. In fact, I enjoy the country so much that I've even opened an office in Sydney. The people I've met "Down Under" have been anything but down or under, appearing very up, motivated, and ready to go. From the Australians I learned a wonderful phrase used to describe someone whose brain is clicking on all cylinders—they say that person is "switched on." I think that's what we'd all like to be: fired up, energetically high and capable, all the time.

I've heard some speakers discuss their "on" and "off" buttons. I don't have an "off" button. It feels too much like faking it to turn buttons on and off. While others might find it a lot of work to be "on" all the time, I don't. I'm not "on" in any way that's not true to me. I don't need to turn off anything or let it go. This is me, professionally and personally: I'm on; I'm engaged with others; I'm listening; and I'm able to quickly synthesize information, get things done efficiently, and move through the world in a zone of Yes! Energy, doing less, making more. I live one authentic, integrated life.

Being in constant energy does not, ironically, *take* a lot of it. What it does require is being constantly supported by inputs that buoy my energy and my optimism. This includes guarding myself against the bad energy of negative people or situations. It's the inputs, versus the depleting, energy-sucking outputs, that can make all the difference when it comes to having ∞EOE∞.

The Energy Roller Coaster

As you know from your own experience, some things augment your energy; others deplete it. Similarly, some things bolster a positive attitude; others topple it right over.

While many inputs and outputs are obvious to us, there are some of which we're not even aware. These are stealthy little saboteurs. In order to have a life of fulfillment and abundance, we have to be aware of these energy depletions so that we can defend against them.

Throughout this book, we'll uncover and examine those things that can add to or take away from your energy and optimism. These assets and liabilities weave their way constantly through your life. Awareness is the first step. It's important to identify and integrate the inputs and be vigilant about and dismiss the outputs. These factors must be accounted for in order for the *Energy Equation* to be effective.

There are many resources that can support, and impediments that can detract from, extreme optimism and energy. These include the following, to list just a few:

Energy & Attitude Assets

Self-awareness
Authenticity
Genuine friends
Close family
Faith
Spirituality
Certainty
Confidence
Connecting and engaging
Money
Purposeful/fulfilling work
Efficiency
Persistence
Clarity
Love
Significant relationships
Sex
Sleep
Nutrition
Good health
Integrity
Grace
Vitality
Hopes and dreams

Energy & Attitude Liabilities

Fear
Hopelessness
Pessimism
Negativity
Isolation
Ignorance

. . . and yes, the following are liabilities, too, and
we'll consider these in later chapters:

Perfectionism
Comparing and despairing
Gossip
Judgment
Confused contexts
Hero complexes—"I can do it all . . ."
Rescue compulsions—". . . and save you, too"

This is one sheet you don't want to balance. The goal for energy and attitude resources is to have all assets and no liabilities.

I have a lot of energy and attitude assets. I'm in constant energy. It's one of the traits about which I'm asked most. Whether I'm onstage in front of a large group, one-on-one, or with a small circle of friends, I'm leading the room with my energy. In fact, it's that very conversation in the room that fuels my energy. It's a cycle. I'm charged by the ideas and thoughts of others, which in turn spark my own insights from my intuition and experience. A great mentor of mine once said, "Believe in others until they believe in themselves." I get excited by the potential inherent in people, and this pushes me to the limits of my own. All this increases my energy even more, which pushes my capacity, and there I go: I'm off and running.

Which doesn't mean I'm not calm and can't relax. One of the first things, I think, that surprises people about me is my general sense of calm. Although I'm moving fast, I'm not frantic. I have, at my core, this sense of knowing, a certainty. The source of that is 100 percent faith based. This is not a selfish act. I do this not just for *me*. As Doreen Virtue puts it: ". . . one person at a time leads to a world of peaceful people, which equates to a world at peace." I focus on my faith because I believe that being one with Spirit means you are loving and peaceful, and that's among the most generous things a person can do for this planet.

I also believe that prayer lies not only in asking, but in listening, a sourcing of energy and optimism. As my mentor and friend Bob Proctor puts it so lightly and so well in his book *Born Rich*, God is not "some cosmic bellboy who is supposed to run and fetch and then deliver." Proctor goes on to define the power of prayer by explaining that "everything you see in this universe, yourself included, is nothing but the expression of an infinite power. This power is forever flowing into and through you. Scientists will tell you that everything is energy. I choose to say that everything is Spirit." The strongest energy in the room always wins, and that energy is sourced by Spirit.

To help me stay in Spirit, I need to find time for my faith. Which means I also need to protect my energy, my focus. Although I'm in what seems to be constant forward motion, I'm also at ease in that I take time, usually in my bed early in the morning, to meditate, pray, and think. My bed is a sacred space for me to connect. It's also a time I pray for those who attack me and my business. This came in especially handy when I was dealing with the lawsuits I described in the last chapter. The negative energy of the people acting in a way that did not resonate with my values was not helpful to *my* energy, so I did two things: (1) I prayed for them, and (2) I asked my team to help shield me from their words and attacks. I find prayer, and the support of my team, to be much more fruitful than letting others cause me frustration. God helps me be calm as I approach each obstacle. Spiritual thought, conversation, and exercises are a helpful source of energy for me.

Also, I like sleep. I find that this is another great way to keep my batteries fully charged. Most people say sleep restores their energy, but I keep myself pretty well "stored up" through the *Energy Equation,* so I never fall far enough behind to require restoration. But what I do is *protect* my energy. Sleep is great for "me" time, really—something few of us ever get. Plus, I enjoy it. Rest is vital.

My environment is also key. I love the water; I love the mountains. I also ski, work out, and run. I like to cook at home with my family; eat out with friends; play with my kids; or write, with my kids, in our gratitude journals. All of these activities are relaxing to me. Even while engaged in them, I remain with my fuel gauge on FULL.

Leading a Life

Since the person with the most energy is leading any situation, I am always leading my life . . . even when I'm not always the leader. Several years after my son was born, I got married, had a beautiful daughter, and went through a divorce. I'm now the single mother of two fabulous children, and as every parent knows, with my kids I'm often *not* the leader. But as every good parent also understands, I am always *leading* my children. Similarly, there are times when, while I'm still leading my life, I follow others. If I think I can learn something, which is often, I allow myself the opportunity to absorb their energy and generate electricity from them.

It's a constant flow. If you surround yourself with smart, switched-on people, the energy stays strong and spirals up.

That's why energy and optimism are the most important factors in leading a life of freedom and fulfillment. *Energy wins, and attitude connects.* That's it, clear and simple. If you lead with motivating, directed, and committed energy—and you maintain a perspective of calm, certainty, and optimism—you can achieve each of your objectives.

Leading with the strongest energy is not to be confused with pushing an agenda. The problem with the latter is that, many times, an agenda is inflexible. That means the person with one is missing out on a lot of valuable stimuli and perhaps inconspicuous opportunities. If you take the time to lead by listening—and I mean sensitive, high-level listening (which I cover later)—to a room, you can control the energy of that room to achieve good results for *everyone* in it.

I like to be in maximum energy leading my life, even when circumstances try to slow me down.

Staying Up "Down Under"

On a trip through Australia, talking on various stages, I found myself with a tightly squeezed schedule and events that went late into the evening. One day I had an early-morning flight from Melbourne to Sydney for a presentation on what I'd consider a fancy stage. It required the nicer end of my selection of outfits. There was a decision to be made: (a) sleep less, and wake up early to get all decked out for the stage; or (b) sleep more, not get dressed up, and do my prep and makeup on the other side of the flight. Believing more sleep to be better than less, I went with *b*.

Well, we arrived in Sydney, but our bags did not. (Reason number seven to opt out of commercial travel whenever possible.) I looked at myself. It was summer there, and it was steamy hot. My jeans stuck; my shirt clung; the humidity was wreaking havoc with my hair; and, to keep it all so pretty, I was sweating, which is really nice. Perhaps I could have dismissed my self-criticism, but my son was there to tell it like it was. From the not-so-proper mouths of babes: "Mom, you look like crap." Always a real confidence builder.

I had to be onstage in two hours. When we realized that the luggage was not coming off the carousel, one of my team members sprang into action and called the hotel to arrange for me to get my hands on hair and makeup products quickly. That we had under control. But clothes were another matter. Apparently, there were no retail shops on our way to, or near, our hotel. In fact, we were informed that the only boutiques between where I was and where I was going were back in the terminal, beyond security. I realized that in order to dress appropriately for the stage, I'd have to make my way back through security even though I'd already left that area.

I dug deep into my Yes! Energy. Now I just had to figure out *how*.

I scouted out security. It was tight, of course. Not "no shoes, no liquids," TSA tight, but tight nonetheless; and the retail shops beckoned from beyond. I grabbed one of my trusty, switched-on teammates, and, fortunately, he was in full "Down Under" Yes! Energy, because after an emphatic conversation with the security personnel, we were able to make our way back through to the stores.

At that point, I had two hours to get onstage. And it was way across town.

There I was, with this guy on my team, who now was on very intimate terms with me, throwing clothes over the dressing-room door. The saleswoman was looking at us like we were crazy, which, in that moment, we kind of were. And so what did we do? Well, of course, we shared our crazy, switched-on energy with her.

Soon enough, we were all in conversation. We talked about what the saleswoman was doing there, her work, her family. Then she asked me what *I* was doing, and I told her about our stages and what we teach.

"Oh, you're like one of those people in *The Secret?*" she asked. When she found out I was actually featured on that DVD, she got very excited.

And so, what did I do? I peeked over the dressing-room door and said, "I'm buying a bunch of your clothes here; why don't you buy my 3 Days To Cash workshop from me?"

The next thing I knew, she was swiping my credit card and my teammate was taking her details for follow-up and writing down her number, *on his hand,* for our workshop. That's leading the room, that's high energy, and that's switched on. Heaps of fun.

From Here to Energy

But how do you *get* here? How do you capture the *Energy Equation* and make it part of your life? Extreme optimism and energy, $\infty EOE \infty$, are achieved by . . .

(1) . . . *changing the conversation* . . .

(2) . . . and sourcing a greater power by creating a commitment of *faith* that fuels . . .

(3) . . . *confidence* and . . .

(4) . . . *certainty* . . .

(5) . . . spurred on by *dreams* . . .

(6) . . . then excavating inherent *gifts* . . .

(7) . . . and cultivating *team* . . .

(8) . . . and engaging the proper *sequencing* . .

. . . to propel yourself into $\infty EOE \infty$.

The *Energy Equation* is simple and straightforward. The more you read about it in these pages, the more obvious it will appear. It will subconsciously seep its way into your life and become part of your actions and thoughts. For example, once you start to *change the conversation,* you'll begin to have a deeper, more beneficial understanding, in every situation, of intention and context than you'd ever thought available before. The goal of the *Energy Equation* is to help you consider your perceptions, shift your actions, and change your beliefs. By taking *action*, you will change your *experiences,* which will then provide *evidence* that bolsters your *confidence,* to propel you into the happiest days of your life.

The *Energy Equation* can be applied at any point in life, at any position along the spectrum of energy and desire. Its key factors are covered in detail throughout this book. If you have a small situation that needs to change, this concept can be applied, and the change can be made. If you have a big dream you want to pursue, this equation will help you get there.

Let's get to it. . . .

CHAPTER 2

The Inquiry:

What's your best source of energy? What/who adds to your energy? What/who depletes or represses it?

The Exercise:

1. Consider the last time you felt naturally high and optimistic.

2. Consider the last time you felt exhausted and frustrated.

3. Consider the people with whom you were involved during these times. Did they add to or take away from the positive energy? Did they help try to turn around the negative energy, or did they exacerbate it?

Next Steps:

Clean up all past messes or let them go. Call or connect with:

1. Someone you recall adding positively to a situation

2. Someone whose energy you admire and would like to emulate

Write down what made you feel optimistic and energetic in these conversations.

BECAUSE
I CAN

The Formula for Forward Motion

The solution to a life that's too busy and unproductive, too cluttered with "have to" instead of "want to," is clear. It's Yes! Energy. In order to free oneself from stress and frustration and create a life of ease, grace, and abundance, one must tap into . . .

The *Energy Equation*

$$\{\Delta C + [F(2C)*D] + G + T\}S = \infty EOE\infty$$

Simple, right? And no math. I'll break it down:

ΔC. *Change the conversation.* (*Delta*, Δ, is that cool symbol meaning "change." *C*, of course, stands for "conversation.")

[F(2C)*D]. Source from *faith* to build *certainty* with *confidence*, driven by *dreams*.

G. Add your own unique *gifts*.

T. Get the right *team* in place. Which includes a supportive community and others you can model for success.

S. Properly support everything by *sequencing* the right thing at the right time.

As a result, you'll have:

∞EOE∞. *Extreme optimism and energy.*

These components are the framework for this book. The *Energy Equation* is covered throughout, and all of the formula's factors are explained in their respective sections.

As I said, these factors work for anyone, in any situation, big or small. For example, if you're someone who is generally happy and content, but you have some frustrations at home and with work, the first thing to be done in order to begin improving your situation is to *change the conversation*. Take a look at what you are doing and the situation . . . and uncover what matters versus what doesn't, what's true versus what's misleading, and what's authentic versus what's getting you out of step with your integrity.

Consider, too, what type of conflicting conversations you are having, perhaps saying one thing and doing another, throwing judgment that you don't pass over yourself on others. This can be very subtle—you might not even realize it—so it's important to examine it. A good exercise is to think about a standard to which you hold someone, and how he or she may be falling short in your eyes. Then think about yourself, and if *you* meet that standard. If you do, consider if you meet it all the time, in every situation. It's a great way to let go of judging others and to hold *yourself* to a higher standard. It also helps you to consider what you're saying versus what you're doing.

The change will be toward having a more positive, energizing conversation, which will then shift your actions and behaviors, and, ultimately, your view.

Then you need to draw upon your *faith* and build on that foundation, through experience and action, to shore up *confidence,* a word that literally means your belief in yourself. It's time to take a step back to truly understand your own belief system, to ensure that you have the *certainty* to make the change you desire and that it comes from a core of calm and knowing. Often, if you retrieve your *dreams*—the desires you let sit on the shelf too long—and make sure they align with your values, you can move into a great life.

The next step is to dig deep and recognize your own talents and skills, to find the inherent *gifts* you may be overlooking or taking for granted. By focusing on what you do well, you'll stop wasting time doing things you are no good at anyway. You will do less and make more in every area of your life. Then, no matter who you are, you need a *team*, in the form of support and community, so that you stay in the Yes! Energy. Even if it means making sure you have at least one friend or colleague who can have the same conversation you're having.

Too often, people surround themselves with negativity, not even realizing that the naysayer is depleting their energy and drive. Team is one of those factors of the equation that will show up throughout your process—as I said, perhaps even when you discover a like-minded colleague as you live out loud in your intention. Your team supports the entire equation, even if it's not yet fully formed, as you move through changing your conversation, sourcing your faith, finding your confidence and certainty, recalling your dreams, and recovering your gifts.

Then, by doing not only what you need to do but doing those to-do's at the right time, *sequencing,* you can speed your way to success, any way you want to define it.

Who You Are and What You Want to Be

Just as the *Energy Equation* begins with changing the conversation, it helps to start by asking yourself some questions, which can lead to a new conversation and set the process in motion. By addressing each of the components, you can establish where you are and where you want to go, and then start to see how to get there.

Let's drill down into the *Energy Equation* using an example from one of my seminars.

1. Changing the Conversation

Max was 34, married, with two kids. His grandfather started a plumbing supply and service company in Lutz, Florida, from which his father had recently retired and which he now ran. His wife worked part-time as a medical assistant in a doctor's office.

We had a conversation about his work, his family, and his life in general, with the rest of the audience listening in.

"It's hard on my wife and kids—I'm working all the time," he said, right off the bat. "Nights, weekends . . . all the time." This is a classic example of someone buying themselves a job, rather than owning a business.

"Why?"

"Got to make a living." He shrugged. "My dad did that, my grandfather—that's the way we do it." Obviously, for too long Max had accepted the mentality that he had to work hard for his money.

He needed to change that conversation. It would start with the people with whom he was surrounding himself. Also, Max needed to believe that money came easily, not hard. That would begin his shift. We'd get him on a faster path to cash and help him retain more of what he was making, so that he could spend more time with his family.

2. Faith

Max and I talked a bit about his faith. He seemed uncomfortable sharing. "I have a strong religious background," he explained. "I'm not sure I'm spiritual, though, but I'm working on that."

"How?" I asked.

"Well, I'm going to go back to church."

"What about talking to a higher power? What about prayer?" I inquired.

"Well—"

"What about carving out 30 minutes every day, maybe in the morning or at night, to check in with Spirit?"

His eyes lit up; he got it. "That would give me perspective, wouldn't it?"

"You bet."

3. Confidence; and 4. Certainty

"What do you want to do?"

"What does that matter?" Max said. "I'm doing what I do; that's what I do."

"Why do you do what you do?" I asked him.

"I have to—it's all I know."

"If you could do something else, *anything* else, what would you do?"

"I don't know. I'm good at this," he said.

"But Max," I replied, "who better than *you* to get what you want?"

"Ha! What?" He couldn't even comprehend that. This was so classic, again. Max knew what he *didn't* want, but he did not know what he wanted . . . so here he was, sitting on a big pile of stuff he didn't want.

"What about your family life?" I asked. "How do you want that to be?"

"The way it is, is the way it is . . . isn't it?"

We had to work on his confidence and certainty. We talked a little bit more about his faith, his core beliefs. Then we got back to his business, the business model, and how he got paid. It was soon evident that he had no marketing plan, his pricing was archaic, and he was underselling his goods and services.

"Max," I said, "you'll never get paid what you're worth."

"Don't I know it."

"But you *do* get paid what you negotiate," I pointed out.

This got him on his heels, but realization set in quickly, and he nodded.

"You need to know what you want, be committed to getting it, lead the conversation, and go get it," I said. We had some work to do on his certainty and confidence. "And so your frustrations at work are that you work too much, and your frustrations at home are only that you're not spending enough time there?"

"Right."

"Is it relaxing to go home?" I asked.

"No," he admitted. "There are a lot of chores to do, and we're always driving the kids here and there. I also bring work home."

This family was not valuing their time together. I had to jump to the concept of team here, because gathering a team is essential to Yes! Energy.

"Do you have help at home, Max?"

"Help?"

"Do you and your wife do all the chores yourself?"

"No, the butler does a little." He chuckled.

"That's so far from what I'm talking about," I replied, turning to the room. "Ever spend $20 at the local diner after work?"

"Sure," Max said. "Easily."

"What if you spent $20 a week for a neighborhood kid to mow your lawn?" I suggested. "Help him start his business? And what if you spent $40 a week for someone to clean your house?"

"That would be nice," he commented.

"Sixty bucks a week, $240 a month," I said. "You can generate one extra service job to make that each month."

"Sure."

"And you could use just two of those extra hours to market your business better every week and get even more jobs to pay for more hours at home. Let's even say that one of you had been mowing the lawn and one of you cleaning the house at the same time, so of the six hours, two overlap. Well, I just got you four extra hours, every week, for you and your wife to be together calmly in your home, where you're not cleaning or doing yard work."

"That's pretty good," he said. "I didn't think about it."

"Because we *don't* focus on it, and so we just let life happen around us, and live in chaos," I addressed the whole room. Unfortunately, too, in many cases, when people clean up that period of time, they'll let some other chore or activity suck up those hours. *It takes focus and dedication to exchange busy hours for productive ones.* Max could spend those extra hours marketing his business, generating more cash, and buying himself more free time. He could also spend several of those new hours being calm with his family.

"Would you describe your household as calm?"

"Ah, no," he said.

"But you want to spend more time there?"

"With my family I do, and, you know, make our home more relaxing, I guess. Maybe look at how we all spend our time together."

5. Dreams

"Okay, so what do you want?"

"To work less."

The man had forgotten how to dream. "I mean, what do you *want?* What's your dream?"

"My wife and I want to take our kids on vacations, and have less bills. Maybe a new car."

Well, that was a good start. Even dreams have to start somewhere.

6. Gifts

"Where do your talents lie?" I asked.

"I'm a good plumber," Max shared. "And I manage the supply store well."

"That's your *job*," I said. "What are your *skills?*" People often confuse the two, so I wasn't surprised by his answer. "Besides the actual plumbing, what makes you good at what you do?"

"I'm reliable, you know, dependable and resourceful. And I've always been a clear thinker. I'm pretty efficient, I think. And I'm organized," he added. He was getting the hang of this.

"And how about away from work?" I asked. "What are your gifts?"

"I'm pretty sure I'm a good father and husband."

"Why?" I prompted, throwing him a bit off balance.

"Why?"

"Those are titles, labels," I said. "What are the skills, the talents, that make you a good husband?"

"Um, well, I'm a good listener."

"Really?" I whispered, quietly.

But he heard me. He smiled and nodded. "Yes."

"That's a gift; that's a skill," I said. "What else?"

"And obviously I can fix things," he said. "Wives like that in their husbands."

"Yes, they do," I replied. "But now I'm bored."

"I'm attentive, Loral," he said, with a little blush.

"More interesting, but not a gift you share with everyone, I hope."

"Um, no," he acknowledged. "I was trying not to be boring."

"Good, I like the action there," I said.

The next step for Max would be for him to understand how he could *use* the gifts he was *uncovering* to help him shift and improve his life. In the *Energy Equation,* Max could harness his natural skills and talents to make more money faster, which would then help him work less and spend more time at home and bring abundance to his family.

7. Team

I asked Max about his home life. "My wife is proud of me and believes in me," he said. "And we have great kids. *Fun* kids."

"That's supportive," I said.

"Maybe we could spend more time together. We have a lot of activities; we do a lot of stuff. I'm with my friends a lot, too. But they're not what I'd call supportive in the sense I think you mean."

"Which is what?"

"Well, when I have some ideas, like business, things to do, even coming to this seminar . . . some of my friends think I should leave well enough alone, you know?"

"I do know, Max," I said. "You need to get better support around you. People who want a better life, too. It's nice that you followed in your dad's footsteps, but if you're going to fix and grow that business so that you're not working weekends and nights, you need to find a mentor who has the type of business you want so you can model that and move on in your life."

8. Sequencing

Then we went over sequencing, how Max went about doing the right things at the right time. That would take some defining and untangling.

I've found that a lot of the students in our community think *sequencing* is a tactical word, and they like it, but often they're confused by it. Yet it's very simple and straightforward. Sequencing is being clear about the right steps at the right junctures. Many moms are actually a great example of this and come to it very naturally. They get up, pack the lunch, get the kid dressed, make breakfast, check the homework, and get the kid out the door to the bus. For many, it's almost instinctual.

In business and in personal lives, too many people plan first, then make a move. As a result, they plan, plan, plan, and never *move*. Yes, we need to plan and organize the content of ideas, but action has to happen first. Market the idea, then make it. That's been a sequence of success for many entrepreneurs.

The path from where someone is to where he or she wants to be is all about discovering the right steps, and aligning them in the proper sequence.

Some of Max's first steps would be to:

- Uncover his skill set;

- Look at exactly the person or business he could model and copy;

- Surround himself with other positive-energy people who have wanted and found change;

- Gather those who know how to do what he doesn't and create a team of them so he doesn't have to waste time doing things he doesn't know how to do or doesn't want to do; and

- Learn how to *earn* away from the job.

But these were just the start. The *Energy Equation* would help Max shift his perceptions and actions and pivot onto a better, more fulfilling path.

Max's sequence of the *Energy Equation* was very specific. For him, it started with, as you see in #1, changing the conversation. Then, he considered his gifts, his dreams, his faith, and his confidence and certainty, and found his team to move forward.

It went something like this:

In the midst of having a new conversation, Max knew he needed action. He realized that his gifts—his ability to listen, being organized, and being reliable—could help him market and build his plumbing business.

The next few days after our seminar, he talked to several of his loyal commercial and residential customers and found out that they needed help with the general upkeep and repair in many areas of their buildings and homes and were willing to pay a retainer to someone who could manage that. Then he met with and talked to some strategic partners, such as the contractors and maintenance workers who came to his supply shop, and found out that they—and their partners, such as electricians and carpenters—were always looking for pipelines to new business.

With a new vision of what his business could be, Max sought out similar models, some in different industries even, and asked their owners for advice. Soon he had a mentor he could talk to about his ideas.

Simultaneously, Max reconsidered his dreams—from the big, such as where he'd like to be in a year, to the small, such as what he'd like to be doing more of, and less of, daily. He took time every morning for spiritual guidance, using his faith to gain confidence and certainty.

Consulting with others and building his team, Max was on his way to spending less time at work (*do less*), while increasing his income (*make more*).

Eager to leap into action, Max decided he'd try out a few ideas, even if they weren't fully thought out or perfect. He knew he could fix and polish them later, once he'd at least tested them in the field. He quickly created various relationship-building programs with customers and strategic partners so that they would pay him up front for products and services that he would provide throughout the year. He marketed—mostly through flyers, referrals, and word of mouth—his all-inclusive home-maintenance contracts to customers, while also selling his network to partners who wanted to joint-venture.

Eventually, Max built his customer base and engaged several partners. In short order, he, personally, was doing fewer plumbing jobs and mostly managing this new type of business he'd created: consulting, overseeing, and supplying products and services for commercial and residential improvement, maintenance, and repairs. He even hired a software developer to create a proprietary system to organize all of it.

Max's knack for efficiency had him spending less time at work and more with his family. With the additional income, he employed the concept of team at home as well, and soon he and his wife had more time with each other and their children. That was a happy day.

And Max was just getting started. Once you learn how to use the *Energy Equation* to get into Yes! Energy, it's contagious. Max would never be the same. He was energized and optimistic. He continued to create new conversations, source his faith, feed his confidence and certainty, pursue old *and* new dreams, and engage a community of supportive teams.

Forward Motion

I've been lucky, because I engaged my Yes! Energy even before I understood what it was. When I knew that I wanted to have my first child and others were telling me it would be difficult to build my business and be a mom, I dug deep to find the conversation I wanted to have, to consider my dreams, to use my gifts, and to find support. Because I've sourced spirituality from a higher place, I had what Deepak Chopra in *The Seven Spiritual Laws of Success* hits on as the "quality of *intention* on the object of *attention*." This gave me the flow of energy to move forward with certainty and optimism. Because I came from this place that was bigger than I was, I went full-court press on my goals and then benefited from what Chopra calls the "organizing power," which then, in my mind, fueled the flow of good vibrations to "orchestrate an infinity of space-time events to bring about the outcome intended."

Because I knew what I knew, I could do what I do. Which sometimes meant *committing* to *what* I knew I had to do before I knew *how* to do it. That's always been my way. *I say yes to opportunity, then figure it out later.* How? By finding those who know how.

When I was in college, I started a personal-training business, which really took off when I graduated. I was very professional about my business, analytical even, to the point of creating a rate-of-return ratio on making people healthier.

Then one day I got an odd phone call from a man with a funny accent. "Hi, I'm callin' from Nu Oleens anda wanna you to worka gas 'n' ol."

"Excuse me?"

This time, my brain's little translator must have turned on, because then I heard:

"Hi, I'm calling from New Orleans, and I want you to work on gas-and-oil rigs." Although that still didn't sound quite right. What did I know about gas or oil? He then mentioned his company, which I'd never heard of. We didn't have its gas stations in Nebraska. I later discovered that it was, in fact, legitimate. More than legitimate. This was a Fortune 500 energy company.

He continued: "And so, you want to come to New Orleans?"

I was intrigued. "Why?"

"We need a health-and-wellness plan for our oil rigs," he said. "We want to consider you and your company for the contract."

Having never been to New Orleans, I said yes and had faith I'd figure out how later.

When I got off the airplane, several executives met me on the tarmac. They led me to a van, handed me steel-tipped shoes and a hard hat, and drove me to a helicopter. We then flew offshore. I don't know if you've ever seen the offshore world of oil rigs, but it's like a little city out there. Among the first things I noticed from my vantage point in the helicopter were these huge vats on the outside deck of the rigs. I pushed my headset microphone. "What's in those?"

"Lard," one of the executives answered.

"What for?"

"To cook with," he said.

"Cook with?"

He looked at me, concerned. "You know, food?"

I smiled at him. Did they really need Sherlock Holmes to solve this mystery? But he was stone-faced, so I just nodded. *Well, sit back and relax on this one, Loral,* I thought. Who was I not to find the easy answers?

We landed on a few of the rigs, I talked to several of the employees, and then we flew back to shore. The man who'd called me didn't waste any time explaining the situation. "Look," he said, "we have all these rigs, and men, and we need nutrition and fitness centers on all these rigs."

That's certainly progressive, I thought.

He went on: "It costs us $60,000 for every back injury. We need to do this, and we want you."

I was shocked. I was 24 years old. I had no clue. How would I do this? I mean, ditching the lard was one small idea, but I knew it would take more than that. I couldn't even make heads or tails of the contract they gave me. Except for the paragraph that said the budget for the project went well into eight figures.

What did I say?

"Absolutely. I would love to do it."

With no clue as to *what* I was doing, specifically, I jumped into running a multimillion-dollar project for a huge international conglomerate. I set out to find those who did know how. I found experts, gathered a team, and got the job done.

I had nothing on my side but ∞EOE∞. I'd changed the conversation (ΔC). I believed (F), and had a huge amount of certainty and confidence (2C) that I could do this, and it was a job that could get me to my dreams (D). I knew my gifts (G) for leading the project and found a support team (T). Then I sequenced (S) by doing the right things at the right time: $\{\Delta C + [F(2C)*D] + G + T\}S = \infty EOE\infty$.

∞

I've since learned that that is enough to tackle any project. The *Energy Equation* begins with a shift in how you perceive and engage in life. That requires changing the conversation, as we'll explore in Part II. . . .

CHAPTER 3

The Inquiry:

What are the best things in your life right now—home, work, friendships, spirituality, experiences, or environment?

The Exercise:

1. Reflect on the past 12 months, and list three events you'd consider highlights.

2. Do these three situations fit under the categories you listed as the best things in your life right now?

3. How can you shift the emphasis of your life to have more opportunities to encounter these situations and the people involved? Ask: "What do I want in life?"

Next Steps:

Begin to consider how the *Energy Equation* can frame these situations and help build more of them. Consider one and fill it into the formula: $\{\Delta C + [F(2C)*D] + G + T\}S = \infty EOE\infty$.

ΔC What was your perspective on the experience? (*Changing the conversation.*)

F How did the experience fit with your belief system? (*Faith.*)

2C In what way did the experience make you feel good about yourself? (*Confidence* and *certainty.*)

D How did the experience help you get closer to the way you want your life to be? (*Dreams.*)

G What skills or talents did you bring to the table in this event or relationship? (*Gifts.*)

T Who else was involved? (*Team.*)

S What was the sequence that led up to having success in this endeavor? (*Sequencing.*)

∞ E O E ∞
Part I: The *Energy Equation*
Summary Inquiry

1. Create a future, imagined situation for which you can fill in the factors for the *Energy Equation*: $\{\Delta C + [F(2C)*D] + G + T\}S = \infty EOE\infty$.

2. As you go through the book and learn each section, you should come back and be able to plug in the variables of the *Energy Equation*. But for now, fill it in ahead of time, just as an estimate, a guess. This will help get you thinking about how to apply the formula to any situation. By the end of the book, you will be able to fill it in for various choices or next steps in your life.

3. Can you change the conversation? What is your old conversation? What's the status quo at work, at home, and in your community? Is that okay, or is it bothersome?

4. Do you have certainty and confidence? What do you feel when you're at your best? How often do you feel that? What's your source of calm? From where do you draw strength? In what do you have faith? What sits at your core, deep down—what's definite for you? What do you know for sure?

5. Can you list the people in your life who support you? What would be your dream team? What does "community" look like to you? How do you wish it looked?

6. Do you know your gifts? Instead of identifying with the actual career or line of work you're in, think about the skills you use on the job, and name those. What about skills you use at home or work that come naturally to you, but for which you aren't necessarily paid or expected to perform? What comes easily to you? What are you great at? What do you enjoy doing that you're able to do without a second thought? What have others said they appreciate about you?

7. What are your dreams?

8. Do you know how to sequence the steps necessary to approach and succeed in most situations? If yes, what's the first thing you need to do to accomplish your next task or goal?

PART II

A NEW
CONVERSATION

$$\{\Delta C + [F(2C) * D] + G + T\}S = \infty EOE \infty$$

"It was impossible
to get a conversation
going; everybody was
talking too much."

— YOGI BERRA, BASEBALL
PLAYER AND MANAGER

MORE
MEANING,
LESS CHATTER

What in the World
Is Everyone Talking About?

Most people are having the wrong conversation. Or conflicting conversations. Or worse, no conversation at all. We continue to live in old models of making a living, education, relationships, and fulfillment—and they just don't work. I'm not sure they ever did. History has always had one constant among humankind, and that's frustration. Many have always been, and continue to be, tired and unsatisfied. That type of living can and should end. Living is an action. We can all do it better.

One of the reasons why we don't get what we want is that we don't *ask for* what we want. Out to eat with some colleagues, I had a relevant experience. Once everyone's dinners arrived, one of the people at the table compared her less-impressive plate of food to her neighbor's. "I didn't know you could get chips with the fish," she said. "Was that on the menu?"

"No," explained the woman with the chips. "I just asked for it."
"You can do that?" the first woman replied.

We all looked at her, somewhat stunned. A woman we knew, who was sitting right in front of us, wasn't aware that she could ask for what she wanted, that she could, literally, order off the menu?

Talk about having the wrong conversation. In fact, many times, people are more likely to state what they *don't* want, rather than what they *do* want. Maybe because it's so easy to do so. I hear it all the time: "I don't want to work. . . . I don't want to be single . . . I don't want to be so unhealthy . . . I don't want to be saddled with all these bills . . . I don't want to spend my whole life not getting what I want . . . I don't want to be so stressed-out all the time."

Too many live in fear, feeling lucky just to be able to order what's on the menu. There is no reason to undercut our own chances for success. We limit our lives, our choices—everything. We're constantly setting boundaries, more clear on what we don't want than on what we do want.

History has proved that human beings are incredibly capable. Look at all that's been accomplished, good and bad, by people on this planet. Yet, in their wildest imaginations, I wonder if the cavemen would have conjured up cathedrals, or pioneers would ever have predicted space travel. Accomplishments were never easy; success always came at a price. Galileo was suppressed, Madame Curie criticized, and even Elvis was told to go back to driving a truck.

A new conversation means a solution orientation, which means *no-limit thinking.* This is the idea that we emphasize possible over impossible, creative over fixed, new over traditional. No-limit thinking means we ask: "Why wouldn't I?" and "How can we?" rather than wonder *if* we can. It's breaking the rules, as sourced from Spirit and in a positive energy, and making "Because I can" your mantra.

Reconsidering the Chit and the Chat

When I was 17, I knew I wanted to do things differently. For some reason, the idea of making money was of immediate interest to me. Some people might find that odd, but for me, it was a calling. Although people can pooh-pooh the idea of wealth all they want, I knew that a person with a lot of money can do a lot of good. I've never seen a poor person give a million dollars to charity! Money plus virtue and positive intention can be the root of a lot of good in this world. With this interest in money—this fire in my belly—goading me, I knew I needed to have a new conversation, one that would explain to me something about how wealthy people got to be that way.

And so, at the fine and curious age of 17, I went to the local bank and decided to pose that exact question to its president. After we talked for a little bit, I asked him to mentor me and introduce me to the wealthy people at the bank.

"Yeah, right," he said. With something of a smirk on his face, he escorted me politely outside. I went right back the next day, and the next. Finally, and perhaps just to get me out of his office, he hired me as a teller. From there, I started to ask more questions, and meet more people.

The lesson? With persistence, and certainty, you can change the conversation and move into action toward a big life. I was getting my certainty from a higher power, so I knew that I was moving forward, solution oriented.

That, unfortunately, is unusual.

The routine of life, the pattern, goes something like this . . . we're born; meet our families; go to school and hope we get educated; and after 18 years or so of incubation, are on our own, thrust into the prospect of making a life.

Okay, so that's the short version. But regardless of how you got to where you are, something along those lines happened to you.

Now, here you are, in a life most likely not of your own making. What's difficult, too, is that you know, deep inside, that you have the ability to create a life so much better than the one you're living. I'm here to tell you that your gut is right. Regardless of where you started, obstacles, poor decisions, or where you are now, you *do* have the ability to create a great life of grace and abundance.

In order to do this, you need to change your view of the world and how you act in it. It's that simple. And in order to shift this perspective, you need to have a new conversation. Because for hundreds of years, people have been having the same conversation, and for too many residents of the planet, that's just not working.

Here's a little look at what happened in the past. People were on Earth trying to figure things out. They had caves, rocks, perhaps a slingshot. They hunted; they gathered. Families, tribes, and villages developed. Different groups met. Sometimes it was friendly, sometimes not so much. They traded stuff and ideas. They fought over stuff and ideas.

Now, jump ahead a few hundred or thousand years, and look—it's the same conversation. We're still a planet of villages trading and fighting with each other. Nothing has changed. Only we've added layers. Few of us produce our own food, clothes, or shelter; and some make a living without creating any goods or services at all.

Basically, we humans have been having the same conversation year after year, millennium after millennium. Despite periods of enlightenment and renaissance, far too many people still go through life just trying to survive, suffering through depression and anxiety, encountering hardships, and struggling with the unknown. Although after a hard day's work, some of us go home to modern appliances, high-definition televisions, and central air instead of a fire, cave paintings, and no front door, survival has been pretty consistently stressful since the dawn of humanity.

Okay, so now that we're all caught up, how can we change that? How can we live lives of ease, comfort, grace, abundance, and fulfillment?

We need to do three things: we need to change how we *see, talk,* and *behave* in the world. In other words, we need a new conversation.

The Weight of Words

Changing the conversation, unlike most things in life, is actually easier done than said. Believe me, I've done it. I was brought up living the same story most of us have been told. That's the problem—that story is negative and depleting. Too many tell a tale of working hard, fighting over scarce pieces of pie, measuring themselves against the rulers of others, living in fear of others, and settling for "good enough." This is the wrong story. But again, that's good news. Because all we have to do to change our lives is change the story. This requires a new conversation, and a new conversation requires a new vocabulary.

— For example, the concept of *scarcity* has to go. This idea promotes a negative, competitive state of mind. Few things are truly scarce, except when they're hoarded. Those who think there is too little actually create a world of too little. They end up creating demand for one small object, and then fighting over that object. That's unnecessary.

What works is to believe in, and desire, that which is abundant. It goes back to high school. Remember the boys who would fight over that beautiful girl, or the girls who would battle over that all-star boy? At some point, this girl and boy were pronounced popular, their stocks went up, everyone wanted to "buy," and their stocks went up again. Yet, as we know in hindsight but sure as heck couldn't see then, all the jostling and frustration were unnecessary. It was, more likely than not, that inconspicuous boy and girl who really had it going on. The teens who could see past the cluttered story of scarcity and find these riches were the ones who benefited.

The new conversation is about expansiveness. And abundance. Those who work together to make the pie bigger, rather than fighting over that last piece, are all rewarded.

— Phrases often need be turned on their heads, too. The idea of *I'll believe it when I see it* might do well to shift into *I'll see it when I believe it*. There's fortitude in faith, and forward motion from fortitude. As Michael Bernard Beckwith suggested in his book *Spiritual Liberation,* it's important to "not dismiss or discard the revelations and insights that have knocked at the door of your awareness."

The solutions are always there. When the database and accounting systems blew up on me, I didn't—I *couldn't*—really believe that could be the end of my business. I knew that I'd have a big, successful company and that the day's events didn't resonate with that vision. There had to be a solution, but I didn't have it. Obviously, I needed to find a better source to cultivate it. I needed to lock in and listen to God.

Usually, if we don't see the solution, we're looking in the wrong place.

— Another word I don't like is *retirement.* Look it up. *Merriam-Webster's Collegiate Dictionary* describes it as a "withdrawal from one's position or occupation or from active working life." I've also heard it called "going to pasture." The online *World English Dictionary* defines it as "seclusion from the world," as well as "the act of going away or retreating." The word *retire* is defined as "to recede or disappear." Withdrawal, seclusion, retreating, going away? Is that really the goal toward which we all want to work?

The new conversation is about next stages, renewal, and growth. Those who have the good fortune to be able to stop doing the work they have to do shouldn't retire. They should move on and up to something better and more exciting.

— Then there's the whole world of *deprivation.* We budget our finances, restrict our food intake (are there uglier words in the English language than *budget* or *diet?*), repress our desires, suppress our emotions, tuck away our dreams. Yuck. We labor under the perception that we must cut ourselves off from anything that's pleasurable. In the money conversation, it's popular to suggest we "save for success." We can't save our way to success. It doesn't work. Low interest rates plus inflation create less cash, not more.

The new conversation is that we can have some of everything that's fun and good. In the money conversation, we must "create success," not save for it. We can build bigger, risk-managed, resourceful, expansive, creative, productive, no-limit-thinking lives.

These are just a few examples of what's not right in our current conversation. I'm sure you can think of several more that fall into this category as well.

Out with the Old Ways

I'd like to knock down a few more institutions and concepts. . . .

Education

What do we learn in school? Granted, I think the social component is important, as is the ability to read and write. But the practical lessons seem to be missing, and we lose our creativity and intuition with too much structure. It would be nice if in six years of elementary school, a few hours were put aside for creativity and philosophy, as well as practical lessons in areas such as basic psychology and human behavior—or my personal wheelhouse, money and investing.

My company holds workshops and seminars on how to make money and start a business. Once in a while, kids join us. During one weekend in Orlando, Florida, for instance, an eight-year-old participated with her grandmother and brother. Not only did the young girl learn MBA-level business and finance, but she was fully engaged and attentive, for three full days. Instead of spending her weekend watching TV or playing with a mobile device, she was interested, and learning. It was quite satisfying.

And it makes sense. Look at all the kids who create lemonade stands. Kids want to learn and engage with each other, even if it's just to build a clubhouse. An education system that kick-starts curiosity and the pursuit of practical knowledge could push our youth into productive behaviors and use of their time, and maybe even spur an important innovation . . . or several.

Jobs

Most people don't give it a second thought: the goal is a job. That's the only choice, the only option. That's sad. People don't have fixed potential; why do they settle for fixed income? Another conflicting conversation. Or people want to make money, but they won't talk to anyone or ask for the cash. *That's* a conflicting conversation. Or someone wants to be literate in the ways of wealth, but won't invest in that education. That's another conflicting conversation.

Fixed income does not equal financial freedom. Nor do fixed conversations or capped educations. But Yes! Energy can, and often does, result in financial freedom.

There is so much opportunity to create and develop in this world. I don't understand why we box ourselves in. It's an industrial-age conversation to believe that we have to do what's always been done, to work the farm or the factory . . . or sit in traffic to and from the cubicle. But we can't make other choices if we don't know them. A new conversation is required.

It begins now. Start with sourcing a greater power, assembling a team, being solution oriented, and getting in your Yes! Energy to attain ∞EOE∞. There are ways to make a living beyond a wage-earning job. When people work together to create their own companies, based on their own ideas, that's a new, exciting conversation. When people work together to create whole new, life-supporting ventures that go beyond business, beyond that which anyone has even yet conceived, that's outstanding. That's a new conversation.

I've seen it go even further. Think about the economy. Originally, economies were micro-communities of villages bartering. Now there are so many moving parts that we don't know who's supplying, who's demanding, and who's creating unnecessary work to collect extra fees. I'm certain that if groups of people got back into creating and innovating and sharing their services with each other, these microeconomies would change the world. In our company's 3 Days To Cash workshops, we do exactly that, by encouraging people to exchange their skills and talents in a mutually beneficial environment.

Guess what? Every single person who walks in the door makes money. Each one. Guaranteed. In fact, we actually *do* guarantee it. That's a new, expansive, inclusive flow of money . . . and that's a better conversation.

Families

This conversation is changing every day, despite and because of *us*. Just look around: traditional two-parent households; single parents; and various gender, extended-family, and generational combinations. I'm a fan of the tribe myself. It really does take a village. Although I am a single parent, my kids are nestled in the core of a consistent and reliable inner circle that nurtures and supports them. These are family and friends of mine whom I trust to support my values and objectives. I'll get way more into this in the team and community chapter of the book; it's a new conversation I believe in passionately.

Investing and the Stock Market

It's time to blow the lid off of Wall Street. The venerable institution is the Emperor's New Clothes, and it's high time someone played the innocent child to shout out that Wall Street is, indeed, naked. The problem is, there are so many who have a stake in the existence of the stock market that those willing to blow the whistle are doing so in the wind.

Now, let's be clear on this conversation. Of course the public markets make some sense. There has always been a need to match those who need money with those who need a place to put their money. Usually new ventures are on one side, and institutions and individuals are on the other, with the market players as middlemen. Back in the day, if a whaling ship were headed out to sea and needed funds to support the crew, why not have a few investors provide cash and receive a share in the bounty of the hunt if things went well? I'm all for this type of shares outstanding in a venture.

The market, though, is no longer that. It's a sporting event, complete with 24-hour-a-day pundits analyzing, commenting, and in many cases, *rooting for* its ups and downs. The party line for those with a vested interest in the machinations of making money out of money is that the markets provide liquidity and facilitate growth in the economy. Maybe they did (and in a small part, still do). But for the most part, now there are just way too many ingredients cooked into the stew. While stocks and bonds and commodities were always vulnerable to manipulation, derivative products—that is, the investing products that don't even have assets to back them up, but are just derivatives of other investment vehicles—can really muck up the whole mess.

If you have no idea how the various public markets work, it's only because you haven't educated yourself by learning the vocabulary. The markets are not that complicated. But that's the way the investment banks like it, because they make a nice tidy profit off of: (1) their customers' lack of understanding; and (2) more important, their customers' reluctance to betray that lack of understanding.

Taking Advantage of "I Don't Know"

Many people are afraid of saying something dumb. Few like to admit they don't understand. Sometimes, even sophisticated people engage in deals, make trades, pursue investments, or just generally go along with things they don't understand. While it may be okay to watch television without a clue as to how the images make their way into your living room, it's not okay to buy a financial instrument or invest in an asset you don't "get."

The lesson? Consider a new conversation where you directly invest in transparent assets and don't rely on the blind, assumed expertise of others without making sure those "experts" have your best interests in mind. That's why a team is so great. The experts and professionals you bring onto your team and in your community should share mutual intent and interest.

$$\infty$$

I encourage you to start your new conversations by considering as many embedded "always been done that way" habits as you can. Consider everyday little "always-have-beens," and then move on to the bigger ones. Thinking this way is a good start to changing the conversation.

And the next thing you know, you'll realize there are no rules. . . .

CHAPTER 4

The Inquiry:

What truths do you hold to be self-evident? What parts of your life have you never questioned? Are there things about your upbringing, childhood, education, work, or relationships that you've just taken for granted because they fall under the heading "That's just the way it is"?

The Exercise:

1. List three things that bother you about your life, but that "just have to be that way."

2. List three things you desire in your life or avenues you wish you could pursue, but that you believe to be unattainable.

3. Write these down again, but invert them (state that the things you don't like are no longer part of your life, and that the things you want, are). Take a moment to consider these new thoughts, and see how it feels viscerally, in your skin, to test and flip these thoughts.

Next Steps:

During your next few conversations, listen carefully to the words being said and write down as many clichés or phrases that seem to be rattled off mindlessly, even perhaps irrelevantly.

Test out the breaking of an idea or institution, whether you believe in it or not. Play devil's advocate and bring it up in a conversation. Gauge the reactions, and write down your thoughts.

CHANGING
THE RULES

CHAPTER 5

Having Your Pie in the Sky, and Eating It, Too

Late one afternoon after my kids had finished their days at school, the three of us were riding up Powderbowl chairlift on Heavenly Mountain. The sun was inching down toward the horizon, but we'd already completed six good runs. This would be our last, which was just perfect. It had been another happy day.

There was a fourth skier on the quad lift with us. He asked if, like he was, we were on vacation. I told him this was our life. "Had to follow Mark Twain," I explained.

He looked around. "Did I miss signs for the Mississippi?"

"To obtain the air the angels breathe, you must go to Tahoe," I recited, paraphrasing Twain.

"Ah, that's nice."

"And true."

"Wish I could just up and do that, move here," he said, head back, filling his lungs with mountain air. "Man, I would love that."

"Then do it," I advised. "We did."

57

"I can't risk it." He shook his head.

"What's the risk?"

"Up and move to a place just because I want to? I have obliga-tions—you know, my work, kids," he said.

I glanced at the two bodies between us. "What do you think these are, mannequins?"

He grinned, but shook his head. "I'm not a trust-fund baby."

I tried not to laugh, although I'm sure I snickered. "I grew up in Nebraska on a farm; put myself through college; started and grew my own businesses despite repeated attacks, libel, lawsuits, and outright lies; and—"

"And? There's an *and?*"

"You bet," I said. "*And* I'm a single mom . . . of two." I pointed to the obvious, sitting between us. "Though you can bet your ski poles, they've got trust funds, actually companies they own inside of trusts, which is even better—but that's another conversation."

"Wow," the visitor said, smiling. "How'd you do it?"

∞

This was not a novel conversation. I have it on airplanes, in retail boutiques, at restaurants—just about anywhere—all the time. Fortunately, I have an answer for most of these people that comes from my own experience. After years of struggling, trying to achieve and prove myself, I learned a wonderful truth: I could change the rules and make up new ones. So I did, and that's how I found Yes! Energy—this easy, graceful, simple way to do a lot less and achieve so much more. Because I was willing to change the conversation and make new rules, I found my freedom. I achieved daily happiness that includes a beautiful family; a trustworthy, re-liable group of friends; a bountiful, productive work community; the best health, sex, and energy of my life; and constant opportu-nities for abundance.

The good news is that since I missed the truth all those years, I understand why others might be missing it, and I've built a busi-ness on helping them find it.

Dirt, Sweat, and Leftovers

My first glimpse that difficulties are often created and not inevitable was as a child living on my family's farm. That 6 A.M. wake-up call for chores was a jolt to my spirit. I'd spend those dark, cold mornings either tending to the animals or the grain or walking the beans. To walk the beans meant to weed every stalk. Every single stalk. Hunched over, sweating . . . it was not my favorite activity. This fun time was then followed by some serious elbowing of one older and two younger (although much bigger) brothers for my sister's and my share of whatever food we could wrangle. It crossed my mind more than once to hoard some ahead of time to avoid the battle.

Although brought up to be mindful of my parents and the family order, my tender young brain couldn't help wondering why all this early-morning drudgery—followed by mealtime chaos—was necessary. As it was, I already had an issue with the whole idea of breakfast, lunch, and dinner. I still do. I mean, who decided that? Why don't we just eat when we're hungry?

As you can probably surmise, I wasn't, and I'm not, much of a mindless rules follower. Oh, at first I followed the rules all right, because, like most little girls, I was eager to please. But I sure didn't do it mindlessly. Eventually, I didn't do it at all.

I decided early on that there needed to be a new conversation. Perhaps a few new rules. I definitely needed to be doing more of what I wanted to be doing and less walking the beans. That's where I found my purpose, helping people get into Yes! Energy.

I do the work I do, entrepreneurial leadership and wealth-building education, because I'm charged, by a calling, to help others live easier lives. Just like doctors are called to heal and teachers to educate, my mission has been to stop suffering and help people live easier, simpler, more abundant lives.

The Impact of Money

One question I get a lot is "Why money?" I had other professions and businesses before starting my organization Live Out Loud. One of them was personal trainer, because I understand how important it is to be healthy and be well. Early on, though, I realized that if people were wealthy, they could do a lot more with their lives—expand their options, including ways to be healthier and happier.

While money may not be the most important thing in life, it certainly can have the most impact. That's why education in pursuit of financial freedom has been my focus. The only difference between those who have money and those without it is that those who have money know the key to generating and maintaining wealth, and those who don't, don't. As in every arena, education can save lives. That's why I go around the globe and teach, sharing the truth about financial freedom.

I also felt that I had no choice. I'm on a mission because this path was one I was meant to take. I have a gift, a money telepathy. I can see individuals and their skill sets, their natural talents, and connect them directly to their fastest path to cash. It's so clearly visible to me, like a "connect the dots to the dough" instinct. It comes, of course, directly from what I learned myself, but I can tailor it specifically, and many times uniquely, to each and every person I meet. It seems I didn't really choose money. It chose me.

∞

My experiences have helped me develop the exciting ideas and actions that allow me to lead a life that's calm, fulfilling, productive, and fruitful. It takes a new conversation, and sometimes changing the rules. If the man on the ski lift wanted things to be different, they could be. But he needed to make it happen. His concern was that it was too risky when, in fact, he was actually risking his whole life by not seeking its rewards.

I'm always examining the rules and many times creating new ones. That's the vital spirit of an entrepreneur. For many, changing the conversation starts with actually *recognizing* rules. We do so many different things for so many different reasons, most of them ones we're not even aware of. I started turning this upside down pretty early on when I was bucking up against breakfast, lunch, and dinner.

Since I've moved along my path to abundance, I've had the opportunity to really consider established rules. In some cases, I had to dismiss them.

For example, when I had a corporate job right out of college, I wondered why I should wear high heels and pantyhose just because that's what women were expected to do in the decade when I entered the workplace. That seemed ridiculous, and it was uncomfortable, so I didn't do it. Of course, I was also written up in my job at least a dozen times. Breaking rules was not looked upon fondly in the corporate world. Fortunately, now most progressive companies understand the need to be more mindful when it comes to the rules they establish.

I'm sure when women first entered the workforce, the men were all wearing suits, and the starched women's suits with big-bow-tied dress shirts made sense. Unfortunately, I was in those transition years when women clung to the male dress model but hadn't yet developed their own style. And so there I was, farm girl gone fashion rule breaker. Now, I'm happy as can be in my jeans, boots, and fun jackets. I've never looked back.

Revealing the Reality Behind the Curtain

In order to make *new* rules, it requires a different perspective about *old* rules. In many cases, I retool and shift conventions. Sometimes, merging concepts that appear mutually exclusive—being conservative and taking a risk, for example—is a good start to a different perspective. As you enter into the world of a new conversation, you will find yourself doing the same thing.

Here are a few new rules I created while turning the old ones on their heads:

— **Be conservative *and* take risks.** To many, risk is associated with aggressive behavior. It doesn't have to be that way. Risk taken as part of a reckless need for validation is not healthy. Risk taken as part of a progressive, decisive action, propelled by faith and certainty, is vital to growth. No business or person can grow without it. *Risk + knowledge + education = experience,* which gets you confident, which helps you grow, and expand.

In his book *Against the Gods: The Remarkable Story of Risk,* Peter L. Bernstein explains, by outlining the history of chance, probabilities, and statistics (more fascinating than it sounds), how inevitable risk is to the evolution of humankind. We've progressed from fate-based, static, fearful mentalities to civilizations that can gauge the possibilities of reward for acts of courage and daring. Thank goodness, too, or how else would Columbus have set sail and given those of us in the New World this chance to live in such an exciting, fertile, free place?

Risk is necessary to creation, but it does not need to be an aggressive act. With a lot of thought and preparation, much risk can be mitigated. That's the new conversation, realizing that risk is not, in and of itself, inevitable. In fact, with the proper *sequencing*—doing the right thing at the right time—it can be managed very effectively. As I explain later, when you sequence, you think ahead to what needs to be done. This helps you see the potential land mines before you set them off.

I live a fun life. I ski, travel, try exotic foods, own a bunch of companies, and run a few businesses. But my life's not fancy. In fact, some would find the house in which I live surprising. I didn't spend money on crazy-big granite walls and an ultramodern chef's kitchen. Our family lives in it, it's a home, and it's full of our memories.

I have a life that fits my family perfectly and comfortably. We live in a town near a lake and a mountain that's as close to heaven as you can find on Earth. I've found that I can have it all if I pick the pieces of the "all" I want carefully. Instead of getting myself in a situation with a house that's too big to heat or in need of constant maintenance, I chose a more modest home in a place that's exquisite. Unlike the vacationer on the chairlift who couldn't take the risk to move from the place he "needed" to live to the place he *wanted* to live, I actually took the time to look at the pieces of the puzzle and arranged them in a way to position myself for high reward, low risk.

— **Be deserving *and* accountable.** It's upsetting when someone acts entitled. The idea that there are those so eager to blame someone else for every bad thing in their lives has become an embarrassment to most sane people. We like to think of ourselves as accountable, that we keep our side of the street clean. Yet, we remain a litigious society, with lawsuits viewed as a road to quick riches. At the same time, there seems to be a lack of *deservability,* an idea put forth so eloquently in the Deservability Treatment of Louise L. Hay's *Love Yourself, Heal Your Life Workbook.* People feel they don't deserve the best things in life, yet when they don't get them, they want to blame others. Fascinating, isn't it?

That sense of entitlement and lack of accountability can be very cultural. I don't mean country to country, but rather community to community. I've been in rooms of people where there's a contagion of confidence and certainty to the extent that everyone is comfortable being fully accountable for their own actions. At other times, I've seen the exact opposite: a scary viral energy of blame and unreliability. There's no doubt that the tone, one way or the other, can be set by a good leader in a family, community, or business—even in a large corporation. A motivated culture is best served by those who think they deserve to move forward, and do so with personal responsibility.

I once met a couple who had created a business that generated several million dollars of revenue for them annually. Then the business environment changed, the company became a losing proposition, and the couple was a million dollars in debt. They were devastated and considering bankruptcy. I went nuts on them.

"Sell your way out," I said.

"What?" the woman said.

"How can we?" the man asked.

"You sold your way up and into a multimillion-dollar business," I pointed out. "Focus on making more money, not the debt. Once you have the money, then you pay off your debt."

This seemed so obvious to me. They needed to pick themselves up and start over. Yet all they could see was failure and frustration. They wanted to push the easy button and be done with it. I wouldn't let them. They even tried working harder doing what didn't work. I wouldn't let them do that either.

"Do what you did before, back when you were building the business from zero," I advised. "Only now you have experience, so you can retrace those steps and do it better and faster. You need to put in the time and get back to where you were. Be responsible, and fix this."

Guess what? They weren't even angry with me. They were energized. They had a sense of purpose and pride. I knew they'd get it done. We deserve to do better. We can, and we should.

— **Be in alignment *and* out of balance.** We are taught to find balance. While I'm all for being in alignment with my values and my integrity, I believe the idea of being balanced is misunderstood and causes a lot of unnecessary aggravation. If you're pursuing many wonderful dreams in many aspects of your life, it's almost impossible to keep all of them in balance. In trying to find balance, too many fall even further into frustration and, worse, resentment.

I like what motivational speaker Lisa Nichols, the author of *No Matter What!*, has to say about doing so much for others, balancing your life to balance all of their needs, but not yours. She notes, by way of solution, "When you've been good to you, you'll serve with more gratitude to everyone else."

I measure success by my ability to be present and active in the coaches' traditional eight arenas: *spirituality, health, career, family, fun/friends, relationships, money,* and *physical environment*. I don't live multiple lives. I don't have the family me, the stage me, and the friend me. They're all the same person, dipping into each arena with the same face, the same attitude.

I live an integrated life. My kids come with me on business trips. I have the same view on my passions with my friends as I do with a new client. I act with the same engaged energy when I'm skiing a run knee-deep in powder as I do when I'm starting a new venture. Whether you meet me at an event, in a store, or while I'm watching my kids, you'll meet the same me. I even have a sound and video professional who makes it a rule to only work with people who are the same on camera as they are off. I'm one of the few with whom she's still working.

I can't be in balance, trying to give eight different parts of my life just enough. I like to give more than enough. If some days that means my life is all about one thing, that's fine. To me, it's all the same—my family, my friends, and me living our life. An *authentic,* genuine life.

I'm supported in this by having some places that I shut off to other parts of my life. My home is for my family and friends.

It's very important to feel peaceful in your home. To feel that it's a haven where you can be restored, feel revitalized, and even gain inspiration. Home is my favorite place. But too often now, you go into a home and everyone is on their computers or PDAs, allowing the outside world to infiltrate what used to be a secure and restorative spot. It would be a giant revolution back into the peacefulness of home and hearth if everyone would commit to communication in the house that requires proximity of real, live bodies and brains.

I've watched too many supermoms (and dads) implode because they feel like they have to be all things to all people, to get *it all done.* That doesn't end up working out. It's usually not fair to anyone. Especially the supermen and superwomen. At the end of the day, there's little resolved and lots of resentment. That's why having a team is so important. Those who can feel empowered by sharing the power, who have the certainty not to be controlling (which I'll cover in Part III), can delegate and expand their lives. While being in balance might be the latest catchphrase, being in *alignment* means knowing your values, your intention, and organizing your life to have it all.

Those are examples of new rules. That's changing the conversation. Add that to a strong, purpose-filled energy—and, as you'll see in the next chapter, you'll be on fire. . . .

∞EOE∞

CHAPTER 5

The Inquiry:

What are the absolute truths/rules you hold to be self-evident and that govern your daily existence? (*Examples:* "Money comes easily," "Life is fun," and "Love is grand." Or conversely, "Money comes and goes," "Life is hard," and "Love is a fairy tale.")

The Exercise:

1. List these rules in two columns, positive and negative. Consider all aspects of your life: spirituality, physical and emotional health, career, family, leisure, and so on.

2. Next to the positive rules in your life, write down how they work for you and help you with your energy and attitude.

3. Consider the rules that are negative, and then write down the *opposite* as if it were true. It's okay if these new rules seem invalid or unattainable; write them down. These are affirmations to which you will aspire.

Next Steps:

Post, in a spot you will see every day (on your wall, exercise bike, bathroom mirror, or refrigerator, for example), the rules of your life as you'd like them to be, including the ones that already work and the new ones you'd like to affirm. Consider following the factors in the *Energy Equation*. (*Examples:* "I look to God for solutions," "I live in confidence and certainty, "I use my gifts," "I'm supported by community," "I take care of my body and mind," "I live where I want," and "I have real, true love.")

Read these out loud one to three times a day. Those that resonate are true now. Those that cause stress need to be *pursued.*

THE
FLAMING
TORNADO

Stirring the Pot with a Burning Focus

After I was onstage at a large event hosted by a well-known motivational speaker and business leader in San Diego, one of the attendees—in from Norway, of all places—approached me in the hall. He tugged at my arm, and I pivoted from the group to whom I was talking to face him.

"I've never seen that," he said.

"Hello," I greeted him. "Seen what?"

"I've been to a lot of events like this—I bring my whole company, to educate the sales force—but this is the first time I've ever seen someone turn it around like that."

"What do you mean?"

"Most speakers push their message from the stage onto the crowd," he said. "You do the opposite—you seem to feed off the energy of the room. I think you could dance with whoever you want, wherever you want, couldn't you?"

Dance with whoever I want? I liked that. I asked him to explain the observation a tad more. As he did, I came to realize that I was doing what I've always done. I was a strong front of energy, a gust of forward motion that picked up the positive energy in my path, lit it on fire, and put it back out there again. I was, in fact, just like my friends had teased me when I was younger, a flaming tornado. This guy said I could dance. Well, all right, now I was a storming waltz of energy, which sounded pretty good to me.

Dueling Dual Desires

I'm diligent about not being judgmental, but one thing I can't tolerate in the "new conversation" is anyone who says he is going to do something, and then doesn't do it. That's not going to work. There's no issue if people don't want to engage their Yes! Energy and energize their lives. That's their business. Similarly, I'm not one to stop someone from standing up tall and declaring she wants to make $10 million. And keep a job. But I don't live on Fantasy Island, and I don't think it's productive for others to either.

While visions and dreams can be, and should be, as far-out as possible, short-term objectives and periodic goals must be realistic, or the sequence of steps necessary to catalyze the *Energy Equation* won't work. As long as people reconcile what they say and what they do, then I can root for any objective. But when I see folks stand up and tell me they want something, and then they don't do what it takes to get there, that's just a waste of time.

If you want to move forward and make something happen, and you've mapped out the plan to get there, then you need to do that which it takes to make it happen. There's no duality. What you *need to lead* and what you actually put together must correlate. Challenging the old conversations requires that you stir the pot, not just for the sake of mixing things up, but to actually *make a change*. That requires action.

There's a lot of literature suggesting that introspection and self-assessment are helpful tools of change. This concept is:

"be-do-have." I'm not into that idea. While good thinking is necessary, it's not sufficient.

The key to change is action. Taken daily, it can influence behavior and change thinking. First you *do,* and then you *are,* then you *attain.* The better concept is "do-be-have." Actions create character.

The new conversation requires action. In order for improvement to occur, change must appear in the form of *you.* The spectrum of change is wide. For some, it's reading regularly and engaging in gentle self-reflection. For others, it's getting into all-out "in it to win it" accountable action. For most, it's something in between. For all, the goals should be the same: to achieve calm, grace, and certainty in a life that is generous with its abundance, easier, and more fulfilling. If a new conversation gives you the impetus to absorb and then see a real, productive change in the way you think and act in your life, then you're off to a great start.

I'm not sure that the reason my friends used to call me the flaming tornado is exactly in line with what the gentleman saw on the San Diego stage. I think they called me that because, in their minds—and probably in reality—I was in action all the time. While I wasn't destructive, I know that I did flip over some traditions and upend institutions, catapulting people to results. Change produces heat. Fortunately, most of it was in pursuit of independence and freedom.

For me, that meant creating my own business. That's an interesting twist on the conversation, because so few people seem to realize that they have limited their lives by living in the W-2, the 1099, or even the sole proprietorships. That's not a structure; it's a shackle. If you're in a new conversation to shift your life, then you need to be the CEO of your own world and lead a corporate life, which means you set up entities through which you run your enterprises and your life, so you can do less, make more, and stay in the Yes! Energy.

In Action from the Get-Go

Even as a kid, I was constantly in the hunt to be the CEO of my own life. When I was in high school, in little farm-country America, my siblings and I had a lawn-mowing business. It was a family affair. First my mom talked to all the people in town to market us. Then my dad got the truck out and helped us lug around the mowers to our gigs. We found our niche in a few cemeteries and open lots. No one else seemed to want to do them. I was indifferent. It was work, it was good pay, and my brothers and I were running our own show. It felt great to have my own thing and own a business, and I had the bug. I was intent on changing the conversation.

While some might have suggested that there was no business to be had, or that I was too young to run my own business, I (1) found a niche where there was, in fact, business to be had; (2) found a great team to work with me; and (3) realized that I could change the rules of what had "always been done" to the way I "wanted it to be."

This still happens. My company is called Live Out Loud because we're changing the conversation about money. First of all, we're talking about it. There are too many cultures and communities that discuss money with a hush-hush whisper. I know that money and business and wealth building need to be pulled out into broad daylight and hashed out in full-on discussions.

There's so much confusion around so much of our lives, and a little conversation would go a long way toward clarity. We don't talk about health, sex, relationships, or money. Yet these are some of the most important things in life. Instead, we talk about sports or celebrities, engaged in conversation about others when our own problems are percolating.

Who Can't Handle the Truth?

One of the problems is that some in the mainstream media are reluctant to have this conversation. They think that the general population can't handle it. Having met the general population, I know this is not true. As speaker Linda Clemons puts it, "Everyone does not have the right to speak into your life. You already know that you were put on this earth for a purpose, and a reason. Just like a brand-new automobile, the capacity as to how fast it can go was built in, greatness was already built into you."

We must . . . well, imagine that the auto plant of which Clemons speaks was Porsche or Ferrari, but also know that we can't always listen to the messages that come from outside sources, like the media. They don't have the right to speak into what we know we must do.

A few TV seasons back, I was a regular on a popular self-help talk show. I was brought in to give families a financial makeover. One couple, with four kids, was on the brink of foreclosure and divorce. They actually didn't even know they were about to lose their house until we checked with the bank and told them. They had no clue, no plan, and certainly no dreams left to inspire them.

I came into their lives to organize them. Now, in my world, that does not mean fixing their little bank account and getting them organized. It meant uncovering their true gifts, their natural skill set, and helping them use those skills to create a cash-generating business. We were going to have them commit to, and lead, their own lives. They'd be their own CEO.

Within 90 days of being on the show, they were making $15,000 a month. The producers couldn't believe it, and they said that neither would the audience.

"But it's true," I said. "We have the statements, real cash-in."

"But how'd you do it?" the producer asked.

"The wife was on fire—she was driving it. She started a new online business," I said. "Then the rest came from the husband's business once he got back in gear."

"'Back in gear'?"

"He had done well in the past, but now the economy had knocked his ego, and he couldn't rebound. He needed to realize that he didn't have to land the plane, just course correct."

"What did you do?"

"You kidding? I called that guy every day at 5 P.M."

"And what was he doing?"

"He was on the couch."

"He was on the couch?" she echoed.

"Yes," I said. "The conversation went something like this . . .

> *Me:* 'What are you doing?'
> *Him:* 'I'm tired.'
> *Me:* 'You can't be tired; we have to make money.'
> *Him:* 'What should I do?'
> *Me:* 'Get up, follow the sequence I set for you, and sell.'"

"And did he?" the producer asked.

"Yes," I said. "And now he's making money again, and I can tell you he's not tired anymore."

If you want success you have to move. This family had the opportunity of a lifetime: to get help from a team of millionaires whom they could model and who wanted to help them. One of them seized the opportunity, and one of them sat on the couch. But of course, we couldn't let that go. We wanted results. We gave a friendly little toe-tap to the backside, and soon both the husband and wife were off and going. They were engaged in their pursuit and each other, and their marriage shifted to solid footing.

"Well, it's a good story, Loral," the producer said. "But on the show, we're going to say they made $6,000 a month, okay?"

"No, that's not okay. They're making *$15,000* a month, every month."

"Really?"

"Yes, really," I said. "It's an obvious hit."

"No one's going to believe that."

"But it's the truth."

"Yeah, but America can't handle the truth," she said, without so much as a Jack Nicholson imitation to deliver the ridiculous claim.

The family was angry, to say the least. Here they were, black and blue—yet profoundly proud—from kicking themselves into shape, and they couldn't even share the full extent of their triumph. "I'm raising four kids, putting together websites, making this happen, getting my husband and my family on better footing, and I can't tell anyone?" said the mother. "This is so unfair."

You have no idea, I thought. This is the sort of disbelief my company deals with constantly. We're introducing a new conversation, and few want to hear it. That's why professional athletes and rock stars lose their money as fast as they make it and only 2 percent of lottery winners keep the millions.

When it comes to money, few people know how to make it. Fewer know how to keep it. *Very* few know how to grow it. Yet . . . it's so easy. Money comes easily to those willing to change the conversation, who are determined and committed to moving forward.

Map the Gap

There are a few first-things-first that must happen in order to have a new conversation and move forward to a life of ease, grace, fulfillment, and abundance:

- **First,** we must know where we are, and we must know where we are going.

- **Second,** we must be able to see where we *want* to go.

- **Third,** we should figure out the path we want to take to see *how* to get there.

This is the general starting point I use with most of my clients. We start with a Baseline, a general audit of where we are in life. This usually takes some organization and assessment. Then, to stay motivated and keep it interesting, we jump to the end, to the Freedom Day. That's the visualization of what complete financial freedom would look like, when all your dreams can come true.

In the last of the three steps, we conduct a Gap Analysis and map out a plan to jump over the gap from here, *Baseline,* to there, *Freedom Day.* This Gap Analysis can be used in any situation everywhere in life. (There's much more on this in The Millionaire

Maker section of **http://www.liveoutloud.com**, where you can ask for a free strategy session.)

These three building blocks help anyone establish a foundation on which to build an improved life—whether it's to fix a current business, buy or get in on a new business, better a situation in a career or profession, or make a big upgrade in the way one is living life in any and all arenas. It might be a quick activity to consider where you are now, and similarly easy to consider where you'd rather be. The Gap Analysis, mapping out that road to get there, takes some real insight and thinking. By using the *Energy Equation,* you can fill in the blanks within your vision.

It all begins with *changing the conversation,* learning to upend those things that don't make sense or that create stress because they don't line up with your integrity and values. Then the difference between those who get what they want and drive headlong at their purpose and goals . . . and those who don't and can't . . . is *confidence.*

Once you truly understand how capable and deserving you are, this *confidence,* combined with a calm, faith-based *certainty,* is one of the most powerful factors in changing your life. Plugged in with *team*—a supportive group who believe in themselves and each other and who do what you're no good at, as well as experts who can help and mentors who can be modeled—the formula is on fire.

Fortunately, we each have within ourselves several skills and virtues and characteristics that come naturally to us. These are our *gifts.* When these are uncovered and put to good use, they can take us straight to our *dreams.* The catalyst in the *Energy Equation,* the fuel that drives this engine, is the ability to do the right thing at the right time, or *sequencing.* Each of these pieces of the puzzle supports one's ability to be an *extreme optimist* who can, despite trials, tribulations, obstructions, and opposition, capture a life filled with ease, grace, fulfillment, and abundance.

The *Energy Equation* begins with changing the conversation. But in order to do this, to shift the way you live and see your life, you need the best resource, the optimal source, for all your decisions and actions. . . .

∞*EOE*∞

CHAPTER 6

The Inquiry:

When was there a time in your life, recently or in the past, when you took a specific action that led to a specific, positive result?

The Exercise:

1. Consider a specific goal or desire.

2. How could you apply "do-be-have" to accomplish this goal?
    (a) What would be the immediate action?
    (b) What evidence or result would that create?
    (c) How would that change your view of your life?

Next Steps:

Consider a goal you can accomplish this week. Write down your view of the objective and your chances for success, as well as the immediate action you can take toward accomplishing that goal. (*Note:* Extra credit if the action causes you to leave your comfort zone.)

Take the action, and write down the result.

Now, write down your new view, the new conversation, as a result of the action and results. What do you think your chances are now for success?

1. What vocabulary can you change immediately, today, so that you change the conversation? Do you use disclaimers, such as "might," "maybe," or "if" when you should use "will" and "when"? How can you shift those everyday phrasings so that it shifts the way you act and think?

2. What process do you follow or activity do you engage in— perhaps mindlessly—that actually, when you think about it, makes no sense?

3. Can you think back to a time recently when you did not (metaphorically) order off the menu? How could you have, in that moment, practiced no-limit thinking?

4. What institutions no longer make sense for you? For everyone?

5. What personal ideas or traditions do you hold dear that might be holding you back?

6. With whom can you engage in a new conversation? Do you know someone who will take aim at some "always been done that way" ways? Find that person, and start the conversation.

7. What fills your day? What are the obligations, the duties, the unproductive business that clutters your schedule?

8. What calls to you? What specifically would you like to be doing with your life? Think about this as a wish list—don't edit yourself, but rather name the ultimate vision you see.

9. When was the last time you were calm and content? What were you doing?

10. Think of a few absolutes, definite rules you adopted as a child, adolescent, or young adult. How many of those do you still live by, and why?

FAITH,
CONFIDENCE,
CERTAINTY,
AND DREAMS

$$\{\Delta C + [f(2C) * D] + G + T\}S = \infty EOE\infty$$

"When the
solution is easy,
God is answering."

— ATTRIBUTED TO
ALBERT EINSTEIN,
PHYSICIST

THE KNOWING CORE

Sourcing Solutions Through Faith

Knowing how to lead when you've dropped down to what feels like the bottom is, paradoxically, leading at the *top* of your game. Since I'm solution oriented, I always have the confidence and certainty that everything will be okay. That's because I have faith. In fact, spirituality and the clarity that comes from my faith are my top values.

Faith is at the core of extreme optimism and energy. Optimistic people don't fall down any less than pessimists; they're just quicker to get up. Optimists fall, get up, fall down again, get up, and continue forward with the same certainty they had at the beginning of the trajectory. While there may be bite-size chunks taken from the body armor, optimists still have their core confidence, and that's what keeps them going. Core confidence is certainty, and that certainty comes from the core knowing, which in turn comes from faith.

My life is, no doubt, spiritually sourced. Like many, I've always believed in something greater than us—God. The unknown is, of course, the unknown—the great mystery that caused humans to search for meaning, either through what we call spirituality or through what cultures have codified as religion. On my journey, I've found it best to honor and learn from, without judgment, the beliefs of others, while I refine and understand my own. I don't speculate on absolute truths. I move forward in faith, with respect and appreciation for the spiritual. My faith is a big part of my life and my work.

That's why I think when people meet me, they are often surprised that I'm actually calm and serene. It takes a lot to shake or unnerve me. Someone has to shock me by lying to me or acting out of integrity for me to then wobble a little bit. Of course, then I realize that's them, not me, and I move forward.

Maybe onstage I present with so much energy that they think I'll be some kind of whirling dervish, a flaming tornado. But I'm not. When I engage, I'm high-energy, but it's a calm energy. I want to lift others into action, to go-go-go, to make things happen, to live an energetic and optimistic life. That's ∞EOE∞.

The Fuel of Faith

What's the source of that? Why are some people oddly, calmly serene and others frantic and anxious? The answer, of course, is a belief in a greater power. The flow goes something like this:

Faith → Knowing Core → Confidence and Certainty

Faith gives you the knowing core. The knowing core is what gives you confidence and certainty. This is an outpouring of energy that links from the middle—the faith-based knowing core—outward into the world, in concentric circles of confidence and certainty. It's a wonderful, virtuous outpouring of energy.

Let's take a closer look at each component of the flow:

— **Faith.** It begins with our belief system. The highest level of energy is faith. There is nothing that vibrates at a greater frequency than the greater good.

If you believe that God is good and that there is a greater purpose than anything we can rationalize or imagine, then you have a source for good. The clearer that channel flows—from belief and faith to action—the purer the energy. Pure energy is high energy. It can keep anyone going. Take any of the characters from any narrative that teaches about faith and you'll find that the ones who surge forward, protected in certainty, have faith.

We live in a time of science. Science has proof on its side. We can *see* that which we believe. Yet, at the same time, many of the most rational, logical scientific brains on this planet practice some form of religion. Even scientists admit that there is a gap between what they absolutely know and what they want to believe. That void is filled by faith.

I live in this logic-based world. I'm analytical and give a lot of credence to the objective and the quantitative. But I also have an overwhelming desire to see that which I can't prove. Of course, that's faith in God. In my life, at the speed at which I go-go-go, I don't believe I could be as calm as I am if I didn't draw my energy from my faith.

Faith then feeds the . . .

— **Knowing Core.** Though René Descartes is famous for his declaration "I think, therefore I am," evidence has led me to believe otherwise. Our brains aren't the boss. It's our intuition, our hearts, our feelings—our connection to that vibration, to the source—that define us. When I make a big decision, it comes from my gut. When I know how I feel about someone, it comes from my gut. When I'm compelled to take the next step, pulled toward it, that comes from my gut. I lead my life, and my knowing core leads me.

Many of us are just born with that calm, knowing core. Maybe it comes from loving parents, a religious upbringing, terrific relatives, or a tight community. Others have had to do a lot of work to attain a knowing core and nurture it themselves.

Whatever "it" is, it has to be bigger than *you*. The mission, as it is for most successful people, has to go beyond yourself. If you have that core driving you forward, it provides ballast. And the seeds for . . .

— **Confidence and Certainty (2C).** We've all seen what confidence can do. It can grab the quarterback spot in the starting lineup, put men on the moon, and propel an unknown senator to President. While it's good to be smart, talented, or persistent, none of these characteristics would get anywhere without confidence. Certainty, that sure conviction that one is headed in the right direction, can often be confused with arrogance. Yet true certainty, coming from faith and a pure energy, is never arrogant. In fact, it's actually humble, coming from an open-mindedness about the world and a nonjudgmental acceptance of all the people in it. Confidence and certainty, or 2C, leads from a place of listening, absorbing, and understanding. Those who understand the *Energy Equation* can be both assured *and* flexible and lead their lives to the place of their dreams.

It works, because confidence is the engine and certainty the compass.

If you have this virtuous concentric outpouring of energy from faith, then you have one of the most important factors in the formula. If confidence and certainty do not come naturally to you, then you need to give 2C a welcome foundation and build it. It's essential to extreme optimism and energy.

Now, let's be clear, there are many situations that will test that confidence and certainty. That's when it's necessary to circle back down the chain, to the knowing core, and to faith. Going back to faith helps build back certainty.

Faith or Façade?

Sometimes it's easy to see who has true confidence and certainty and who is, perhaps, carrying around and covering up a core of "empty."

Those with true confidence and certainty are:	Those who have a façade of fake are:
Calm	Absolute
At ease	Anxious
Open-minded	Arrogant
Kind	Blaming
Productive	Uncompromising
Creative	Controlling
Expansive	Insecure
Loving	Mean

Sometimes, though, it's difficult to tell. We've all met plenty of charismatic people who immediately capture our attention. This can happen with colleagues, friends, even lovers. It's especially difficult to see the façade if you fall in love, since, as Shakespeare knew, "Love is blind." Those misjudgments of character and eventual mislaid trust can happen to anyone. I've had it happen to me. I am—we are—after all, human. That's where confidence and certainty come in handy again. Although it would be nice to have "knowing-core x-ray vision" so we could see who is who right away, we don't. Besides, it would take a little bit of the drama and tension out of life, which is often what makes it exciting.

You, like all of us, are susceptible to poor decision making. That can sometimes happen when you're an open and trusting person. Those are good character traits and shouldn't be worked on or worked out. With 2C on your side, you can still be open and trusting, but you can also take action to mitigate poor decision making. This includes other factors in the *Energy Equation,* such as getting support and advice from others on your *team* and checking in on the *sequencing* of both your thought process and actions—thinking things through and putting the right steps in the right order.

I wish I'd done this better a few times in my life—mostly in the "love is blind" category. In my marriage, I allowed myself to lose myself. I fell for a man whose values were not mine. That was a low moment for me. It led to poor choices with my team, and I lost some great friends and business partners in the deal. I created massive contradictions in my life because in choosing him over my community, my values, and *me,* I compromised. The situation gave me the greatest gift, though, because we created a beautiful, amazing, lovely child. She is a wonderful blessing.

When the floor is falling out from beneath you, it might be that you are surrounding yourself with conduct that isn't in line with who you are. I know the range of behaviors I find acceptable. It is the same that I allow for myself. I can't accept anything less.

A System of Values

It's not just that behaviors are behaviors, but they are symptomatic of and governed by beliefs and values. When someone lies, it's not just the lying that's the problem. It means that that person may not value honesty or have integrity, at least in that moment or with you. That's the *real* problem. When your values are compromised because you allowed someone with different values to dominate the energy in the room and to lead the situation, there's no alignment.

How do you know, though? How do you know when a behavior is a little uncomfortable—or a lot—and when you need to change your own or move away from another's?

Certainly, we all have had an occasion where we lied or someone lied to us. It happens. Usually, one act is not going to define character. Although, sometimes, it does reveal it. Most of the time, a bad decision is a learning experience. Mistakes can provide education and growth opportunities. Life offers a long journey on which we can learn and grow, but the easiest people to understand are those who act consistently and clearly with the core values that resonate with yours. My life works best when I surround myself with people who know their values, who stick to their values, and whose values are in alignment with mine.

I have five top values that I hold dear:

- Spirituality.
- Truth/integrity.
- Clarity/creativity.
- Energy/health.
- Grace.

If ever I find myself feeling anxious or uncomfortable—that is, less than certain—it's usually because something has occurred that was, or someone has acted, out of alignment with my values. Other behaviors weren't in line with mine.

For example, when I was told to walk away from the hits I was taking in my business by getting rid of it, I made a vital decision to stand in integrity. Others thought that was a brave and difficult choice. For me, I had no choice. I pay those whom I'm supposed to pay. I keep my side of the street clean. I stand up to, and answer, allegations and objections. I'm amazed how many people refuse to walk through and deal with any mess they've made.

Once I heard someone say about me, "Man, she's really been hit hard, and still she keeps going." I was proud of that. And it's true: If I'm leveled or struck down, I try not to let myself down further by compromising my values. I've done that. It felt terrible. Worse things happened. I'm my best self when I source Spirit, and find the confidence, certainty, and faith that I will get back up. There is a path, and a lesson. I just have to listen.

Conversely, when I find myself feeling my best, it usually means I'm in a place that resonates, and in the company of people who are in sync, with my values.

When we compromise our values, that's a scary place to be. The whole fight-or-flee instinct shakes our cells. It's situations like these that confidence and certainty come in handy.

An Attempted Siege on My 2C

I had two frustrating situations where I needed all the certainty and confidence I could get. My brand and reputation were under attack. I'd taken years to build both, with integrity, and I couldn't allow either to fall. It was essential that I remained uncompromised, even as I was feeling battered and a bit bruised.

— The **first** incident was accidental. At least that's what I choose to believe. I established my company in the 1990s, began using and establishing commerce with the name Live Out Loud in 2001, and trademarked the brand in 2005. The businesses, products, and services have run, in continuous operation, under that brand name, for about a decade. Yet in 2008, the Oxygen TV network launched that as a new tagline.

We gave them a call. Their response was somewhat nonchalant and along the lines of "Aren't you cute? Sue us." After a few attempts asking them to cease and desist, I decided that a lawsuit was not worth my time or money. I wasn't much in the mood to play David to their Goliath. Although I knew with certainty and clarity that we were in the right.

Our team looked for ways we could turn the situation around, use it to our advantage, and create awareness for our own brand. Since the cable channel's social-media reach was quite large, we decided: "If you can't beat 'em, join 'em." While there, we invited people over to our world of Live Out Loud. That ended up working out very well for us.

— The **second** incident, though, was much more insidious and mean-spirited.

As everyone who has ever used an Internet search engine knows, there are companies that promote other companies by slandering the goods and services of the company for which the user was searching. These promotions show up in the form of "scam" and "rip-off" reports on the margin of the search engine's site when the results' page appears, and almost everyone with significant brand recognition is included in these search-engine attacks. A salacious tagline entices the user to click on the advertisement, which then takes the user to the report's site, which then recommends the user go to a competitor's site. The reports come off as polished and credible, stating an interest in the consumer's best interests. Once investigated, however, a nefarious operation surfaces.

The companies, from Eastern Europe, as we discovered, are paid to go on competitors' sites and divert traffic, basically stealing potential consumers. These hijackers don't function totally without mercy, however—and, in fact, if the offended party pays $75,000 to $150,000, they'll remove the rip-off report from the search site. It's an interesting revenue model. The bad guys have two potential streams of income, from both the thief and the victim.

The problems, of course, are many. For one, the reports are captured by consumers and other sites, spreading false rumors. Two, the ads are viewed by every single potential client who goes to the site. Three, some of the clients believe the ads, even if they don't click on them.

The solutions are few. Although a company can try to buy those same ads on their own results page, it's not always possible, as the spots are already purchased; and it's prohibitively costly to outbid. Additionally, the search engines don't (as of yet) have a mechanism for dealing with the problem.

Many colleagues in my industry whom I respect have advised me not to pay the ransom, so to speak. The preferred strategy is to: (1) communicate directly and clearly with existing clients and consumers, and (2) beat the hijackers by generating enough organic traffic to overwhelm these hostage attempts.

Although this attack on brand and reputation was happening to some of the best in the business, I didn't feel any company in my misery. I was offended and angry. It was actually quite shocking to me that someone, anyone, could creep out from behind the protected anonymity of the Internet and "blackmail" me and blacken my reputation and brand. While it wasn't personal, since they were doing it to all the brand leaders in my industry, it was difficult not to *take* it personally. It rankled. These people, these businesses, were acting in a way that threatened my core beliefs, which then threw my perspective of what was fair in the playing field out of alignment.

But we stood up to it. We counterattacked. Again, we did so by getting experts on board who knew how to help us work better with various search engines so that our potential customers could find us without the hijackings.

We survived. I was very grateful for my certainty. My extreme optimism and energy were vital in this situation.

Fortunately, I recognized that the bad behavior was theirs, not ours. Successful people get attacked. Those companies and players were stuck with themselves, while my company and our players got to walk away together. Our values, our certainty, our energy and optimism were still intact.

Forgiving in Order to Forge Ahead

Moving forward with certainty and confidence also requires the ability to do just that: move on. Whether it's personal or business, energy can be depleted by grudges and resentment. Maintaining extreme optimism and energy requires forgiveness. Forgiveness of others when they behave badly, and yes, forgiveness of ourselves. When mistakes are made, we need to take a moment to consider and absorb them, learn from them, and then shake them off and get ready for the next play.

While forgiveness relinquishes blame, it does not dispose of responsibility. In order to nurture certainty, we need to stay accountable. In order to be accountable, we can never, ever compromise values. Certainty can only flourish if we understand our core beliefs and never compromise ourselves.

Obviously, energy and optimism must be defended and protected, as well as nurtured and replenished. My energy is *directed* and *intuitive*. It comes from that core knowing, which in turn comes from faith. My faith nurtures and feeds my confidence and certainty. I also keep my energy going by surrounding myself with the right people, and putting us in optimal situations. My friends and colleagues share similar values, we behave in ways that strengthen our beliefs, and we create an environment that supports our ideas and activities. Although just as the context of our lives can feed Yes! Energy, outside forces can also contaminate our ∞EOE∞.

One of the top rules for maintaining extreme optimism and energy is to *protect* your energy. You cannot allow it to get contaminated by negative energy, full of low vibrations that deplete and misdirect. If you feel this bad energy, you must immediately remove or shield yourself from the person or place generating it. Just as the highest vibrations—the highest energy—have a pure, spiritual origin, the low vibrations attack from a space of darkness and despair . . . and there is no room for them in Yes! Energy. One source of protection is your certainty and confidence, and the source of that is your faith in a higher power.

As we move forward in this unpredictable world, various situations lie in wait to throw us for a loop. It's not if, it's when.

With a core calm, knowing strength, you can commit to leading a life of Yes! Energy, and that commitment can get you through anything. . . .

CHAPTER 7

The Inquiry:

What do you believe in? Think about your faith—how would you define it? Does it provide a knowing core?

The Exercise:

1. Consider a list of values (which are available at **http://www.liveoutloud.com**). Then select your top five by filtering out which of these you absolutely, positively, cannot live without.

2. Reflect on a situation where you felt anxious or threatened. Which of your values were out of alignment?

3. Recall a situation where you felt comfortable and at ease. Write down who you were with, if anyone, and what you were doing. How did the people and the situation line up with your core values?

Next Steps:

If you haven't done so already, find a way to infuse, very specifically and methodically, spirituality into your day. Schedule it into your morning or night. Allocate an amount of time that is doable. Create a commitment to faith by sticking to this schedule of spiritual reflection, conversation, or exercise every day for at least 20 days.

CULTIVATING COMMITMENT

Faith-Based Leadership in Every Situation

My company creates and feeds off of many mantras. Two work especially well for us because we are, and they encourage us to stay, confident and certain.

— The **first** surfaced a while back when our team decided to nix the middleman of "set" and follow the charge of "Ready, *go!*" This charge not only put us into action, but forced us to be confident and certain, regardless of whether we were "set" to do so. This has kept us in action and encourages me to lead the company to move forward with extreme optimism and energy.

When I first got into wealth-building education and I was working with others to learn the industry, something didn't sit well with me. Most of the concepts and coaching were based on theory. There was usually a scripted, general approach that was meant to be "one size fits all."

This old conversation made no sense to me. First of all, theory isn't action. Second, that "one size" usually doesn't fit anyone

93

quite right. Although a widget may be a widget, every human being on this planet is unique. We may have common patterns and behaviors, but we each have a distinct series of experiences that have led us to have our own perspective, on our own path, following our own vision. Everyone has a different problem or mess they got themselves into.

As every entrepreneur, small-business owner, or corporate employee who's ever tried to market a product knows, while you have to balance the desire to customize with the need to systemize, it helps to tailor supply to demand as specifically as possible. Although wealth-building education can be a high-volume business, the best companies in our industry have scalable systems that can focus on the individual.

Feeling frustrated with the way things were and the old conversation, I knew that (1) I wanted to get into this business, and (2) I wanted to change the industry by offering helpful products designed to suit each person's needs. I also had another audacious goal. Basic financial literacy, coaching, and slight life improvements were not enough. My goal was to change the financial conversation and inspire lives. Oh . . . and to make millionaires. I had no idea *how* I was going to do this; I just knew I wanted to do it. Eventually the company did just that—we helped people become millionaires.

— Thus was born our company's **second** mantra, which led to the concept of this book, of course. It was, as I mentioned earlier: *Say yes, and then figure out how by finding the people who know how.* This idea of knowing what I wanted to do, without knowing how to do it, but finding those who do, has been a common story of my life. That said, the story wouldn't work without extreme optimism and energy, supported by certainty and confidence.

The Inevitability of Unpredictability

The world is an uncertain and unpredictable place. Even the best risk-assessment and risk-management professionals, those who have statistics and probabilities down pat, know that there are single events that can blow apart any analytical estimate and send the world scrambling. Those who have certainty in their core can ride the currents.

Good things happen, bad things happen . . . we experience it all. We've all had the unexpected knock us down, we've all lost relatives and friends to accidents and disease, we've all failed. By the same token, we've all had wonderful surprises surface at the most unexpected of times. We've experienced the joys of relationships, the elation of achievement, the wonder of births and growth, the comforts of love and connecting, and the awesomeness of nature and the world itself.

What none of us has ever experienced is the ability to control any of that. That is our context. Although we can be confident and certain as we move through the world, we cannot control how the world moves around us.

There is a not-so-fine line between being certain and being controlling. In order to have extreme optimism and energy, you must lead your life and be in charge of your own decisions, but *certainty is not control*. That's a vital distinction, and an important point about ∞EOE∞. The goal is to lead your life and (a) attain, (b) live with, and (c) spread extreme optimism and energy. That does not mean that every time you say yes, the world will say yes back to you. In fact, many times it says no. Or worse, nothing at all. That's irrelevant. It's about commitment to a solution orientation. The goal is to keep saying yes and keep moving forward with confidence and certainty. If you source *Yes!* from a higher power, then the people in your life, your team, can help you figure out how.

I'm always amazed how many people don't give *context* its due. As a result, they are frustrated, resentful, or worried. Those emotions deplete energy and undermine confidence. When I was getting divorced, I was out of it. I may have—as the result of my situation, my context—made poor decisions. I acted outside of my values in order to compromise. This was bad, bad, bad.

We see people go through hardship and expect them to act the same as they did when times were better. It's easy to be strong . . . when you're strong. What's difficult is being in power and in charge when your world is rocked.

Fortunately, the *Energy Equation* has always helped me, even on my worst days. It's an excellent source of analytics—a reliable plan—into which I could insert my decision making. At any given moment, I could: (1) *change the conversation;* check in on my (2) *faith,* (3) *confidence,* and (4) *certainty,* as well as my (5) *dreams;* (6) consider my skills and *gifts;* (7) gather support from my *team;* and engage these factors by (8) *sequencing.*

Because my context was not usual, though, I needed to allow for that and rely more heavily on other members of my team with better perspective at that moment. Sometimes, taking charge of a situation effectively just wasn't possible, but because I still had my faith, I could muster my confidence and certainty and not worry so much about controlling that which couldn't be controlled.

Staving Off Stress When the Situation Reigns Supreme

Growing up on a farm, I got a quick education in what I could control and what I could not. Farmers work almost every day of the year in an annual cycle of seed, tend, and harvest. They wake up before dawn and do backbreaking work all day. Yet, despite the fact that they can control their schedules, they have little certainty about the outcome.

Although they can manage the risk with some science and the lessons learned from the generations that came before, they can do nothing about Mother Nature, pestilence, or disease. There's just no ensuring the harvest. Hence the huge market in commodities futures, created as a sure-sale exit price for farmers who wish to hedge their bets. Managing risk through public markets is the only way farmers can control the outcome of their efforts. Those who think they can control risk by controlling their environment are operating under outer insanity, not inner certainty.

Stress is when you lose faith and replace it with fear. If you have faith, then you are always certain, although never in control. A colleague of mine arrived in a house of worship to give a talk on inspiration and motivation and went to give her audiovisual aids to the resident engineer. She was directed to a stairway in the lobby, with an arrow and a sign that read: CONTROL ROOM. The idea of a room above with that title, overlooking the sanctuary, made her laugh. Could it be the place from which all of life's events were, in fact, directed—similar to air traffic? Or maybe a "man behind the curtain," an all-powerful Oz-like character who could control fate, dwelled there? Well, of course not, but the very notion, in that place, gave her a chuckle.

The idea of not having control, though, does not mean giving up control. Just because we can't fix an outcome doesn't mean we can't manage risk and probabilities. For example, people who get into business relationships without contracts are taking unnecessary risks. Worse, they're allowing something else, the court system, to be in control of their fate. I don't like to trust the justice system with the outcome of my efforts, so I cross my *t*'s, dot my *i*'s, and make sure that all my business is in writing, on paper. Confidence and certainty are precious factors in the *Energy Equation,* and they need to be maintained and supported with managed risk and due-diligence processes.

If you truly have faith, yet the outcome of an event isn't what it was supposed to be . . . well, then you know that the outcome is, in fact, *exactly* what it's supposed to be, and your objective was not meant to be. Because I have confidence and certainty, I don't allow outcomes, or context, to give me stress. I believe, and I move forward.

The Nonnegotiable Necessity
of Commitment and Leadership

Extreme optimism requires *commitment* and *leadership*. You must commit to faith, to a core knowing. If you don't have it, you need to build it by sequencing the right actions. A supportive team and community can help with this. Those who engage you in a positive, healthy, optimistic conversation will foster confidence and certainty. You cannot allow anyone to threaten your faith. If you find yourself in codependent, depleting relationships, you must end or drastically change these relationships. This may sound harsh, but it's imperative. Nothing is more threatening to your freedom than the shackles of negativity, meanness, and small, scarcity thinking.

Several times a year, I hold Loral's Big Table events. These weekends help establish and nurture a community of wealth builders interested in changing the conversation and moving forward into a life of financial freedom. The team created by these groups supports extreme optimism and energy, and helps each person involved find abundance on a path of ease, comfort, and grace.

During one of these sessions, we were talking about deservability. The discussion ranged from inaction and safety to an earnest pursuit of going after, and getting, what you want. An accomplished entrepreneur and now successful investor from Chicago stood up.

"How do you take it?" she asked.

"What's that?"

"The judgment," she said. "All the people who criticize your ambition, who say you're greedy and arrogant because you're going for it."

"Has that happened to you?" I asked her.

"I'm asking *you*," she deflected.

"The people who judge me don't know me, and I don't know them," I said. "They're uninformed."

"But it still hurts, right? I mean, you're not above it, are you?"

"No, I'm not above it," I agreed. "But I feel worse for them. They can't even imagine going for anything in their life, so they judge me for doing it in mine. They even comment on how I travel with my kids and take them around the world. They sit back and criticize. Like the people who are overweight and say to their friends who've lost weight, 'You're too skinny.' Why can't they just tell their friends they look beautiful?"

"Wouldn't that be nice," the woman said.

"It is for me. I don't have those kinds of people in my life."

"I do. You're lucky," she told me.

"I'm not lucky, I'm leading," I said. "I'm clear, and I'm certain. I don't let them in there. Why do you?"

"I don't really let them in," she replied. "They're sort of just there."

Which is typical of most people. Circumstances dictate choices, which then result in decisions that make up a life. Few people break out of old conversations to question established rules or leave the hand-me-down village to find supportive communities that allow them to create optimal options and lead a new life.

"Why would you tolerate any of that judgment?" I asked. "My family, my friends, my inner circle, and my community—they wouldn't do that. They've seen me in action. They've seen me at work, and when I'm with my kids. They appreciate what it takes for me to go for it. I move away from those who aren't in line with my values, who've changed or compromised, and I surround myself with the right people—a tribe—and structure things in a way that's aligned with my values."

∞

Those who judge other people's lives do so because they themselves are uncertain and grasping for some semblance of control. The whole idea of snooping around in other people's business—of reading tabloids, of gossiping—is not only a waste of time, but it contaminates energy with negativity, which slows you down.

Interesting, too, is the fact that in addition to being uncomfortable being judged, people have a similar discomfort with being complimented. The fear of criticism and the fear of being put on a pedestal both lead a person away from certainty into hesitation and immobility.

When you are confident and certain, you know what you know, so judgment doesn't hurt, and compliments are not awkward. Yet so few people *claim their personal power, or their knowledge of who they are.* In fact, most folks who observe me as I receive a compliment find themselves laughing that my thank-you is usually accompanied by a look that relays agreement.

"That was gutsy," someone once said when I affirmed a compliment.

"Was it?" I asked. It made me wonder if confidence and certainty have gotten lost in that unclaimed gap between arrogance and a false humility. I hold honesty, with myself and others, in high regard. If I've made an effort, through health and fitness, to look better, I'm going to accept, appreciate, and own any compliments I receive.

John Gray put it perfectly in his book *What You Feel, You Can Heal.* He said:

> When you love yourself in the presence of others, you are able to express your inner gifts and talents without fear or restriction. The more you love yourself, the more you are able to come out. The more you come out, the easier it is for people to appreciate the real you, and not the image you project or the mask you wear. The more people appreciate and love you, the more you can love yourself. It is a cycle of increasing love and true self-expression.

Yet, over and over again, people choose to play small, even with themselves.

When you lead your life with confidence and certainty, and not arrogance, you are *your own CEO.* You, the CEO of your life, must be committed to following a mission statement of the type found in various business books. I work off a variation on the idea set forth in *Built to Last: Successful Habits of Visionary Companies,* by Jim Collins and Jerry Porras:

- *Purpose:* This is an objective you never check off. It's the underlying theme, or idea, of your life.

- *Mission:* These are specific short- and long-term goals you check off, in service of your purpose. Collins and Porras named some of these *BHAGs*—Big Hairy Audacious Goals.

- *Narrative:* This is the look and feel of how you move through your journey. This comes to be your identity.

- *Values:* When you lead your life, what you are must be aligned with who you are.

Managing your life with confidence and certainty allows the right energy and attitudes to come in. Extreme energy fuels purpose and identity. Extreme optimism keeps the mission on target. This all expands year by year, as it does for me, through commitment and dedication.

I knew early on what I wanted to accomplish, so I chose a sector of wealth-management education in which few others play—which is entrepreneurship, micro-communities, direct investing, and building companies to lead. My purpose was to change the conversations that people were having about money, create worldwide financial literacy and entrepreneurship, and help anyone, anywhere, achieve financial freedom.

My mission was to direct people to organize and understand their current situation so that they could exploit their own potential and use their abilities to create and establish businesses, organized as legal entities, that would allow them to generate immediate cash. These "Cash Machines," as we came to call these entrepreneurial ventures, would force people to "say yes now and then figure out how." I was certain that if people could get out of their heads and into action, they'd move fast past perceived objections, and into possibilities, even before they actually believed they could. I knew that because that's what *I* did.

The idea for this type of business came to me while I was still in the corporate world. Of course, it wasn't as fully formed as it is now, but the seed was there, and I wanted to get moving on it. Not willing to give up my job, I straddled the divide between my W-2 and my new venture.

I said yes and figured it out later.

I woke up at 5 A.M. to call and coach clients who were on the East Coast. Then I went to work until 5 P.M., came home, and called my local West Coast clients. Back then, I didn't have much of a team (or support, for that matter), only a notion that I wanted to quit my job. I did much of the work myself. My aim was to make enough money, equal to my take-home cash, to validate quitting my job.

Reluctant to go into debt, and not yet ready to bring in partners, I moved in with friends and sold everything I owned except my Jeep and my computer. In eight months I replaced my salary. Then I rented a room, a little office space.

I also remained at work.

I couldn't do it; I couldn't pull the trigger. I was afraid of everything that everyone who faces change is afraid of. I didn't want to lose my health insurance, I didn't want to leave vested money and a 401(k) on the table, I didn't want to be brave and go solo, only to fail. This approach was hesitant and fearful, far removed from certainty and confidence. The funny thing is, though, I thought I *was* certain and confident. The problem was that I wasn't properly sourcing the sacred sequence of ∞EOE∞. I had my faith and dreams, but I wasn't using all of my gifts, finding a team, or sequencing properly.

Now I'm where I want to be because this experience helped me realize that people need guidance, practical tools, and continual support to pursue and achieve financial freedom. Our company provides just that. We direct people to their certainty and confidence.

Now my mission has been accomplished, my purpose sustained. We work closely with each and every committed client to make them all millionaires. The goals are real, not conceptual or theoretical, so they require a lot of personal, tactical, and tangible work.

Since our wealth education is done in the world, not in the classroom, when the economy took a beating, so did some of our clients who engaged directly in specific wealth-building ideas. Our approach has always been a little ahead of the curve, so my colleagues are rarely surprised when we execute our next big thing. Yet many told me they were actually shocked that even after the recession/depression, our company stayed the course and encouraged our clients to do the same.

I am confident and certain that our approach to wealth building, and the education system I've developed to convey that, is the most effective and powerful method for making millions. That's my narrative, and I'm sticking to it.

Sheepology

Unfortunately, many people don't even know when they're not leading their own lives. Although certainty is not control, the reality is that many people *lose* control because they are, in fact, uncertain. Think about that. If you're certain, you know you can take charge and lead your life, without the stress of having to control everything. If you're uncertain, then you rail against the outcomes of events in which you didn't have the confidence or certainty to take the lead.

There are so many influences in our lives that some people think are their own choices, assuming that they are in charge. Yet many decisions we make and the things we do or accept are, because of time and knowledge constraints, based on other people's direction. Our lives require a certain amount of deferring to the lead of others—that is, following. Or, as Martha Hanlon, co-author of *Customers Are the Answer to Everything,* has termed it, "sheepology."

Although some instances call for this, most do not. Too many of us "follow" our way around, navigating our own health, education, and careers. We can go to a doctor, but still manage our own care through research and investigation. We can go to school, without pledging allegiance to every teacher's suggestion. We can find a way to wealth and business ownership that goes beyond the default of getting a job and barely making a living. There are many other situations in which we can lead, if we just commit to saying yes, change the conversation, collect information, take charge, and figure it out.

For some, leadership is associated with stress. Yet it's actually the uncertainty that comes with following that creates stress. By taking charge, you'll find that your life becomes more calm. It also allows you to take more risks, because if you're in charge and operate from a place of confidence and certainty, you can manage those risks. Courage and risk expand life. Caution and fear shrink it. You know from your own experience that taking charge of your choices and shifting the decisions to create an optimal outcome is energizing. Leading through action, with certainty and confidence, is exciting. It increases your engagement. This, in turn, allows you to be more optimistic.

Can you _____ [fill in the blank of what you want to do]?

Yes! is the right answer.

Yes! Energy can get you there.

Now you just need to figure out what it is you really want to do. . . .

CHAPTER 8

The Inquiry:

How do you lead your life? When do you follow? To what and whom are you committed?

The Exercise

1. Examine the last time you felt stressed or out of control. What were you doing? Was the situation, in retrospect, as daunting as it seemed? How could you have stepped out of frustration and into faith at that moment?

2. Write down the name of anyone who you think appears calm and serene. What is it this individual does that makes him or her seem this way?

3. When was the last time you followed others, or the crowd, into a situation that worked out well? What about a situation that worked out poorly?

Next Steps:

Think about a goal that you want to achieve. What part of the preparation could you dismiss in order to move right into action? What immediate step could you take to get started? And who can help you with this?

Make a call, today, to that person to put the first step in action. Then write down what you did to skip "set" and get right to "Ready, *go!*"

DUST OFF YOUR DREAMS

The Driving Force of Desire

Following a fun workshop day where more than 200 people turned a stuffy ballroom into a buzz of activity and excitement, some friends and colleagues of mine and I were sitting around a hotel pool, enjoying drinks and appetizers. We were talking about the energy of the room, and the observed phenomenon of the people there coming in with stress written on their faces and ending the day elated, positive, and engaged. It's quite thrilling to watch and awes me every time.

"I think I know what it is," one of my friends said. "I think it's that they're in action; they know they can commit to and lead their lives—take charge."

"It's true," I agreed. "It's very calming to know you can take charge of your life."

"It's weird," he continued. "When we provide people with the plans to create change, they seem less inspired. But when they're in the room, talking to each other and us, creating community, they're on fire."

"If everyone had the right plan, they could all be on that course," I said.

One of the wiser in our group leaned back and shook her head with a smile. "Well, you know, Loral, Martin Luther King, Jr., didn't stand up and shout: 'I have a plan.'"

Our group went quiet. She was right. Martin Luther King, Jr., had a *dream,* and that's what rallied the world to create change. As effective as plans and prescriptions can be, they're not inspiring. I should know better, too, since I urge all my clients to dust off their dreams and get on their way to building the lives they want. While action can create the evidence that provides confidence, dreams inspire and fuel us to stay in action.

Once past childhood and into the responsibilities of early adulthood, many people lose their ability to dream. Even if they've maintained a capacity for holding hopes, they adjust their desires downward and don't dream big enough. That's sad. If we're going to be committed to, and lead, a life that's everything we want it to be, we need to know *what* we want it to be. We need to know our dreams.

Self-editing your life to cut and paste what you *think will work* into what *will be* creates a smaller life. The goal of ∞EOE∞ is to live an *expansive* life.

That's why dreams are one of the factors in the *Energy Equation.* You can't have extreme optimism and energy if you don't know what you want. You have to have big dreams to drive and source the optimism and energy.

Remembering How to Think Big

If you've forgotten how to dream, consider starting with the idea of *legacy.* For what do you want to be known and remembered? What do you want to leave behind in your wake? What do you want your legacy to be?

I'd like *my* legacy to be that I changed the conversation everyone is having about money. The current conversation has conditioned too many to be protective and fearful, reluctant to take risks. The conversation needs to be that positive, confident *action* can lead to a *result* that becomes the necessary *evidence* to create *confidence*. Those who know this are on their way to a life of financial freedom.

Changing the conversation shifts expectations and actions. That's why it's the first factor in the *Energy Equation.* That's why it's my dream, because I feel that it can help dreams come true for everyone.

A new conversation, one that emphasizes "because I can," leads to a revival of dreams, which fuel energy, shift attitudes, and inspire optimism. Optimism is what makes us move forward into positive action that can make our lives much bigger and better.

What *is* optimism? Is it some sort of relentless hope? If so, how do you establish an attitude of relentless hope? Mark Twain, my Tahoe neighbor, give or take a few generations, defined an optimist as a "day-dreamer more elegantly spelled." There's something to that, to dreams driving hope. Certainty and confidence are directed by a vision. A vision comes from knowing your dreams.

When I was thinking about the moment when my dreams would be realized, I had a vision of a cozy, comfortable home, in a beautiful part of the country where I could play, ski, bike, run, and even play paintball. I'd lived in many beautiful places, close to the vision, but they weren't quite right. Then I was introduced to Lake Tahoe, and I finally saw the reality my dream could be.

Energy, Evidence, and Faith

I've always been optimistic. I think that's because I have:

- A lot of different types of *energy* to collect information and knowledge, with more than enough left over to get into action to pursue my dreams.

- *Consistent evidence* that my efforts pay off, which then gives me confidence.

- A *commitment to faith,* which provides me with certainty in the hardest times and keeps me in an attitude of gratitude.

Different Types of Energy

There are several types of energy, all of which can be generated via various sources for different purposes, and which I cover more extensively in Chapter 10. I have a *directed* energy, which allows me to focus on my goals and drill down into the steps to get there. A big part of my energy is *intuitive,* in that I can sense certain aspects of what's going on in a room without getting clear signals or communication. I can slow the room down, versus watching it speed up around me. When it's at its best, my energy is *present, engaged, aware,* and *sensitive.* It can also be *electric* and catapult others.

Consistent Evidence

What I do works. Not only for me, but for the thousands of people in my community of wealth builders. Trouble is inevitable. What matters is how we *deal with* the obstacles thrown in our path. When we move forward with Yes! Energy, we realize that failure is really success, because failure is where we learn. Through mistakes we create lessons that provide opportunities to do better, and then those opportunities create positive evidence of success, which then bolsters confidence. This formula is helped by practice and repetition—and more repetition. I practice the same "success" behaviors over and over, *patterning my own best self* to carve out a consistency in all of the things I do.

Commitment to Faith

I'm often asked how I can do all the things I do without fear. The fact is, *I just know.* I have that core of knowing built from faith. I'm in daily conversation with God, Whom I can't see and Whose existence I can't prove. My faith goes beyond logic to pure belief. My spirituality is not an intellectual exercise. It's a *cellular-level knowing.* I don't control it, but I do source it.

Being in daily prayer or conversation with Spirit helps keep faith active. This commitment can be cultivated by making time, every day, for contemplation, meditation, and prayer. I also find that by opening my mind to the flow of energy that comes from the highest vibration, I become less controlling and more certain. This sets in motion a fantastic chain of events.

My faith provides calmness and clarity, which allows me to breathe. That ease then gives me a moment to consider that which feels chaotic in my life; to define it; and ultimately to relegate it to the small, insignificant corner of the room. I can then move into *gratitude,* and keep my conversation positive and reinforcing.

∞

Energy, evidence, and faith help me make my dreams come true. Everyone has different dreams, and I believe each and every one can come true. For some people, the dream is smaller and contained. Maybe it's a home with enough bedrooms for all the kids and an oven that works. For others, the dream is huge, such as a business venture that educates preschoolers around the world.

Regardless of the size or scope of the dream, I believe that with the right steps taken at the right time, anyone can make anything happen. Once you understand how to revive your dreams and put them into the *Energy Equation,* you will see how tangible and real-istic dreaming can be. It starts with small, daily goals and builds into the biggest aspirations of all. Let's face it: even if you start out small, all dreams, eventually, should be big.

Dreams drive energy. By keeping what we want at the forefront of our pursuits, it helps energize them. That's why manifesting what we want and nurturing our dreams need to be a daily part of our lives.

Leading and Manifesting

Manifesting dreams begins with manifesting my day. An important component of that is making the morning time in my bed sacred and healthy, sourcing Spirit. To do that, I start with sufficient rest the night before. Usually, I go to bed the same time my kids do, by 9 P.M. In the morning, I wake up fairly early, even before my son and daughter do, and I engage in meditation and prayer. This spiritual realignment can take up as much as the last two hours of my time in bed. Thirty minutes before I need to get up, I do a lot of visualization and consideration of my workday. It's here that I get ahead of myself, *sequencing* the steps I'll take to accomplish all I want to do. When the kids get up, I spend time with them, eating breakfast and talking about, and helping them sequence, their own days.

This thought process works its way into my entire calendar, not just my days. I plan ahead into the weeks, months, and years so that I incorporate all the things I want to do. I like to work in a minimum of 120-day segments—so if I know I have to achieve such and such goals for my work, plus I want to travel with my kids, spend a certain number of days skiing, enjoy personal relationships and time with my friends, and make visits back to my family in Nebraska, I like to frame my calendar around these specific objectives. I also include random flexibility days so that there are times I can go hang out in the ski lodge with no agenda.

This daily commitment to leading my life and manifesting my objectives take energy. The thing is, though, I don't even entertain the idea of being tired. If I need energy, I'll go source more of it. When I'm powering through all that I need to do, I take good care of myself so that little depletes that energy. When I'm in a business meeting, or getting ready for a day of powder skiing, I don't eat junk. Then when the meeting or the day is over, if I so desire, I enjoy whatever food I want. When I want to perform at my best, I eat energy food, the kind of stuff that positively fuels my day. I ski a lot, and I set aside a chunk of every day to do some form of exercise or relax. I create windows for reflection and consideration. I set up my life so I can go to the office for meetings, then come home for lunch or an afternoon snack with the kids.

Sleep, meditation, scheduling, food. These are helpful tools to support my energy and my attitude. I also incorporate the spiritual into my day, every day. It's not just a one-day-a-week affair. I meditate and pray a lot, even within the course of my daily activities. I'm in constant conversation, living out loud, manifesting.

Although manifesting can help you consciously create your reality by visualizing and believing yourself into that reality, it doesn't mean that you can hang out, do nothing, and think happy "woo-woo," "joy, joy," no-reality thoughts. The universe will not provide if you sit on the couch.

This method is also mistakenly thought to mean being able to actually control, out of thoughts and feelings, exactly what you create. In manifesting what or who you want in your life, stubborn adherence to your own perception of what that is can make you miss out on the arrival of your objective. Often the arrival is inconspicuous, and thus dismissed or initially discounted. *2C* of the *Energy Equation* can help manifest dreams, because confidence and certainty allow you to accept that which comes your way with ease and grace. By releasing those old conversations, expectations, and paradigms, you can let those gremlins go.

It's as simple as *ABCDE: A*llow, *B*elieve, and *C*reate; and *D*reams come *E*asy.

The Courage to Create

I coached a client in his early 30s who'd worked in construction for years, but always on other people's houses. The problem, for him, was that although he wanted more, he never saw himself as the builder; he always thought he was the worker. He was very hesitant to talk to anyone about his goals or dreams.

Fortunately, he had a good community and support. Some of his friends had successfully worked their way out of debt and into wealth creation. Eventually, their energy and optimism became contagious. He decided to view himself as the builder, not the worker . . . the owner of a business venture, not the employee. It seemed like a dream, but he started by changing his conversation with himself, with his friends, and soon enough, with investors. He scoped out land and a potential development project, generated interest from backers, and started the venture.

He now leads his own life, and the risk created calm. He experiences less stress and frustration, and has more energy and excitement about life, than he ever did as a "worker." The key for him was wanting to change bad enough to exert the effort to make the change happen.

The choice seems simple. You can stay in a pathetic cycle of poor, unhappy, and afraid; or you can spiral into the virtuous cycle of the core vibration—find your faith, source Spirit, make a decision, and rediscover your dreams. With the right attitude, energy, and teams in place, anyone can start living an easier, more fulfilling, calming life.

∞

Even if the dreams are clear, it's no secret that people limit their potential by allowing negative feelings and thoughts to infiltrate. The judgment of others only fuels that fire.

Most people were motivated, perhaps way back in childhood, to achieve greatness. Yet somewhere along the way, when the dreams were shelved, those optimistic muscles became atrophied little fellows.

The question is, how to rebuild that attitude so that it supports a simple, fulfilled life with no effort at all.

The answer: the constant flow of ∞EOE∞.

The right energy puts your best self into the best things in life. My connectivity is grounded in and sourced from conversation . . .

with my kids, my friends, my colleagues, my clients, myself, and Spirit. When I'm onstage or in the middle of a large group, I open myself up to the vibrations around me and allow the energy to flow to and from me. I'm at my most pure and authentic when I'm a vessel for that energy, just letting it flow.

This may not resonate with everyone. Many people would rather walk the beans at 5:30 A.M. than talk to more than one person at a time. Everyone has a source from which energy flows. Maybe it's from holding your baby, walking your dog, or sitting in a quiet cove at the lake. There are no rules attached to finding the sources for energy, and sources can be different for different people. My suggestion is that you *go to the place where you flow.*

Now, you might insist, *I can't get there. I'm stuck in this life, this business, this day. I can't just up and go down some path in the woods.*

But you can do *something.* The point is that life is about choices. Maybe you have dozens of responsibilities and obligations and too many are too dependent on you, you, you. What kind of story is that? Who'd want to read it? You are here on this earth to have your own story, create your own life.

If the strongest energy always wins, then you need the strongest energy *in order to win.* A great source of energy is the proper use of your gifts, as Part IV explores. . . .

∞EOE∞

CHAPTER 9

The Inquiry:

What's your dream? What do you want your legacy to be?

The Exercise:

1. Take a minute to visualize your best life. What does it look like?

2. On what aspect of that life, of that dream, could you hang a vision so that you are driven and motivated to change your actions every day?

3. How can you fit manifesting into your life? Have you ever seen it work for you? Or for someone else?

Next Steps:

Write down an achievable dream. Consider how you can think about that dream, every day, to support the idea of manifesting it into fruition.

Go to **http://www.liveoutloud.com** and fill in a "120 action plan" with specific actions you can take, every day, to create evidence that you can get closer to the dream.

Make an effort, every day, to cultivate a commitment to faith.

∞ **E O E** ∞
Part III: Faith, Confidence, Certainty, and Dreams
Summary Inquiry

1. What sources you spiritually?

2. Where do you find your calm? When are you tranquil and serene, if ever? And with whom?

3. How do you make time to commit to faith into your life?

4. Contemplate the "knowing core" . . . do you think you have it? Or is there something empty and anxious within you? Do you draw upon fear, or confidence and certainty? What can you do to create a knowing core?

5. Among the people you surround yourself with, who shares your values? Whose values fit with those to which you aspire?

6. When has your faith been tested? What did you do? Did you have control? Did you feel certain?

7. List your core values. Are these in line with those with whom you work and spend time?

8. What do you do to protect, and source, your energy? How can you do that better?

9. How can you commit to leading your life? List the areas that need your attention.

10. What's great about you? List as many traits and points of pride as you can. If this makes you uncomfortable, you're okay— keep doing it.

11. Dust off your dreams—what do they look like?

$\{\Delta C + [F(2C) * D] + G + T\}S = \infty EOE\infty$

PART IV

HONORING
GIFTS

$$\{\Delta C + [F(2C) * D] + G + T\}S = \infty EOE\infty$$

"[S]ociety as
a whole benefits
immeasurably from a
climate in which all persons,
regardless of race or gender,
may have the opportunity to
earn respect, responsibility,
advancement, and remuner-
ation based on ability."

— SANDRA DAY O'CONNOR,
SUPREME COURT JUSTICE

THE TALENT WITHIN

Excavating Excellence from All Types of Energies

We are given everything we need to have the lives we want.

Before you read on, really think about that. It is in you, in your makeup, to be who you want to be. Perhaps conditioning and experiences have repressed those wonderful gifts given to you as part of your creation, but they are still there, and they are still yours.

Each of us has talents and skills that are part of our very being. Even better, each of us has a distinct set of tools that are our own. That's why we're here: to discover, uncover, and use those gifts, and to share them with others.

Many people don't really know their gifts. More amazing is how many *deny* them. And then there are those who don't support the gifts of others. Judgment and criticism can stall a life, yet we often dish it out and allow ourselves to receive it. As Marianne Williamson said so wonderfully well:

[O]ur deepest fear is not that we are inadequate. Our deepest fear is that we are powerful beyond measure. It is our light, not our darkness, that most frightens us. We ask ourselves, Who am I to be brilliant, gorgeous, talented, fabulous? Actually, who are you *not* to be? You are a child of God. Your playing small doesn't serve the world. There's nothing enlightened about shrinking so that other people won't feel insecure around you. We are all meant to shine, as children do. We were born to make manifest the glory of God that is within us. It's not just in some of us; it's in everyone. And as we let our own light shine, we unconsciously give other people permission to do the same. As we are liberated from our own fear, our presence automatically liberates others.

Life is a field of opportunity open to planting seed, cultivating, and harvesting. We need to live it big.

Since you're engaging ∞EOE∞ and changing the conversation, a good question to ask is: *What's the big game I'm going to play?* If you often find yourself tired and in despair, perhaps you're just sick of playing small. I'd even venture to say that your body is rebelling against the decay of your gifts, the fact that you have these wonderful instincts, traits, behaviors, characteristics, and abilities that you're not nurturing or supporting. Gifts are given to us for a reason—to use them.

Now you may be thinking, *What gifts? Loral doesn't know me. I can't sing. I can't draw. I don't have any gifts. What I <u>do</u> have is a job that takes up nine hours of my day, a family that needs meals prepared and the bills to be paid, and a spouse who'd like some attention once in a while. My only gift is that I can get up every morning and get through it all again.*

If this is the message streaming through your brain right now, turn it off. You have no idea how many great gifts you have that you are ignoring, using for small and meaningless purposes, or giving away.

There are too many who undervalue or give away their talents, who treat their gifts as if they are nothing and gratuitously offer them up without reaping the proper rewards. When we use, share, and value our gifts properly, we receive rewards in the form of positive, regenerating energy and optimism. If we give away our value, by extending our skills and talents without getting paid or recognized, it depletes energy and creates a negative attitude. Yes! Energy requires us to uncover and nurture even unacknowledged skills to efficiently source energy and attitude. Gifts, when used correctly, can be superpowers.

Energy Types and the Gifts That Support Them

Let's consider first all the *energy* and attitude to which you should aspire. Then let's look at the *gifts* you have that can help you attain these. I mentioned a few of these earlier, but now let's get into it.

Leading, Directed, Open Energy

This energy is calm and focused. As you'll see in the discussion of sequencing, my purpose is ahead of my output. I consider what it is I want to accomplish and what I hope to transmit to others. Often, I will help my energy with language such as: "What do I hope to accomplish with this meeting/conversation?" before I enter into the situation. By latching my energy onto my goal, I'm pulling toward me that which I want. I'm focused; I hone in. But I also need to be flexible and adaptable to a degree. Balancing the directed with the open requires . . .

The Gifts of Intention and Conviction. This is revealed in many ways. Maybe you were the type of kid about whom it was said, "[S]he sure knows what [s]he wants," because you spent hours on a task or would endlessly attempt to talk your way into something. Suppose, now, that you find yourself often accommodating others, because there is nothing more important than your relationships and your family, and you will do whatever it takes to make it work.

Both of these seemingly unrelated traits reveal a gift of intention and conviction. There are few human beings more exciting than those who have intention and conviction. If ever you've shown the ability and agility to monitor, anticipate, and act so as to accomplish a specific goal, for you or others, that's the sign of intention, and that gift can give you leading energy.

Intuitive Energy

When I'm operating at my highest, all-cylinders energy, I'm sensing the vibrations intuitively. I feel those moments when I'm with my kids; when I'm skiing; when I'm in great conversation; when I'm feeling intimate; and when I'm connecting, even from a distance, with others vibrating with a strong desire to have exciting, supercharged, big lives.

This requires . . .

The Gifts of Empathy and Emotions. I live success and failure through every cell of my body. Unlike those who profess to be compartmentalized with their emotions, I can't do that. Yes, I compartmentalize my workday and events and activities so that I'm efficient and one thing doesn't bleed into another, but my feelings and thoughts are fully integrated. Although I process things logically and act with a constructive mix of thought and feeling, I live every inch of my life, the good and the bad, through my cells, my gut, my very being.

I know I'm not alone, but there are too many people who feel guilty or insecure because they have this constant flow of emotion mixed with their energy. They work to suppress it. I refuse to do that. Empathy and emotion are gifts, and to suppress them wastes the very energy we want to bolster. It's time for those who "feel bad that they feel bad" to stop apologizing for their emotions. Yes, it is possible to be a full human being and have extreme optimism and energy.

Those who don't already own this gift can cultivate it. During an unfortunate visit to the hospital (for kidney stones), my doctor was beyond compassionate. I appreciated his humanity and personal attention.

"Went through it myself," he said.

There it was, empathy through experience. That's how we gain most of ours.

"I'm thinking that should be a prerequisite for getting a woman pregnant," he continued.

"Empathy?" I asked.

"No, passing a kidney stone," he said. "I was compassionate in the room with my wife because I'd felt like I'd gone through something similar."

"Well, sort of," I said, not empathetic enough to betray my gender's claim to the worst pain ever.

Present, Engaged Energy

Although it's nice to be able to multitask in this day and age, there's something very attractive about a person who is present and engaged. This type of energy pulsates through a situation, taking charge by grabbing hold of the moment and carrying along everyone in its path. It's quiet, but not contained; and it has the calm, certain confidence that represents ∞EOE∞. Present, engaged energy pays attention and is able to sense and see what is really going on.

This requires . . .

The Gifts of Awareness and Patience. Life moves at its own speed, not ours. Everything we do seems to have its own timetable. We can't fix the past or predict the future. Yet there are many who live their lives looking back or jumping ahead. Present energy has to be *in* the present. Those who are engaged are "here and now." That's not easy to do. It takes the gift of being aware, and patient with the speed and timetable of life—of being here and not there.

When obstacles present themselves, it's a good time to test if you have the gift of awareness and patience. If you have an overall perception that these trials will not last forever and that better times are coming, you have these gifts. Calm heads always prevail. Usually people in caregiving and lifesaving lines of work have this skill set.

It can certainly be cultivated. One of the best ways to generate this gift is to model those who have it. If others grab your attention by grabbing you with their energy, they are most certainly present and engaged. Spend some time observing them and watch for signs of awareness and patience. Ask them about their views, their habits.

I've also found that those with engaged energy, who are aware and patient, are able to draw upon their faith.

Sensitive Energy

There's a great gift that comes from both instinct and learning, and that's *Level III listening,* as explained in the great book by Laura Whitworth, Henry Kinsey-House, and Phil Sandahl, *Co-Active Coaching: New Skills for Coaching People Toward Success in Work and Life.*

There are three levels of listening:

- **Level I** is listening to yourself and the blast of stimuli. It's mostly noisy and reactive.

- **Level II** is conversation and connection. It's very much in the moment.

- **Level III** is a calm, almost omniscient level of listening where you can hear and understand, and sometimes anticipate, all of the obvious and subtle signals and zero in on the essence of what's being said. People who can engage Level III listening have a sensitive energy. This operates much like intuitive energy, but is anchored more in the external than the internal. It requires . . .

The Gift of Compassion. The gracious act of compassion is undervalued. It's a wonderful thing to see men and women who free their minds, throw off intolerance, and open their hearts to others. There are a lot of variations on the human form, a lot of different paths on this planet, and so many different ways of thinking and acting. A capacity to appreciate this complex tapestry seems to drive sensitive energy.

Compassion is the gift of not forcing logical arguments on others in order to defend or justify, but rather just supporting. This gift opens up the brain and the gut and every cell to feel the surrounding energy and be receptive to the unexpected.

Those with empathy usually apply their own relevant experiences, but those with compassion often reach out without any understanding. They don't have a filter judging and reframing, so they can collect a lot of information and are exposed to many sides of a situation. They serve others. This broadens their experience and, as a result, increases their sensitive energy. Compassionate people will tolerate a lot more of the available options than someone with preconceived notions, narrow views, and biases, so their learning and growth can expand exponentially.

Electric Energy

You've been in the presence of these people. They "light up the room," as we like to say. What is that? What is this fascinating lightbulb energy? It's that "gift" that I mentioned my friend Diane and I would notice—the one I have and you may have. (If you don't, don't worry, you can capture it as well.)

This requires being vulnerable and authentic, as well as . . .

The Gift of Charisma. This gift is fascinating. I'm not sure how you get it, but I surely know who's got it. You don't see it all the time, and when you do, it's energizing to everyone in the vicinity. Perhaps *you* are one of these charismatic people. If you've ever been told that you have this light, this intangible "it factor," it's imperative that you not dim it. Many people with charisma are embarrassed by their own charms, so they hold back when they should be pushing forward.

Many kids have charisma. They have this natural beauty that shines through. Unfortunately, something happens around the preteen years when someone tells them they're too big for their britches, or they've burst out of the norm in some way that made others—their peers or adults—uncomfortable. They are embarrassed—or worse, ashamed—and they start to condition themselves to quash that energy. That's too bad.

In Greek, *charisma* means "gift," and the implication, in the mythic era, was that this came from the gods. If you've been able to hold on to that chain of energy that seems to come from a greater spirit—that comes from above—into adulthood, then that's a gift you must share with the world. Your electric energy will do everyone a lot of good.

Determined, Persistent Energy

To quote Calvin Coolidge, "Nothing in the world can take the place of persistence. Talent will not; nothing is more common than unsuccessful men with talent. Genius will not; unrewarded genius is almost a proverb. Education will not; the world is full of educated derelicts. Persistence and determination are omnipotent."

This requires . . .

The Gift of Endurance. If goals take anything, it's the endurance to be determined and persistent. You've made it this far—you have endurance.

The first 18 years alone take a lot of grit and determination to get through school, both academically and socially. Although many of us may have forgotten the hard hits, we all took them here and there. They say old age isn't for sissies, but neither is being young. Navigating difficult situations, staying with families and friends to work out relationships and hardship, pushing through jobs to rise in a career . . . that's endurance. Yet it's too often ignored, used for small and meaningless purposes, or given away.

Stick-to-it-ness can work for you and against you. For example, my sweet first child took more than 45 hours of grueling labor. Although I may have wanted to leave the room several times, I never did. That worked out well. Although I stayed too long in the corporate world because I wasn't committed to my identity or mission at that point in my life, I had trepidation about leaving a supportive infrastructure, and I didn't want to leave money on the table. I had great endurance that I was overlooking, keeping small, and giving away.

Sure, Genuine Energy

Shakespeare said it best: "To thine own self be true." Each of us is a distinct individual, and there's a reason we're here.

It's your biological and existential imperative to be who you are. If you don't know who that it is, you must find out. This is your identity, the fingerprint of energy that sets you apart. It requires . . .

The Gifts of Authenticity and Straightforwardness. Are you one of those people who sometimes puts your foot in your mouth? Yes? Well, guess what? That's a gift. Although you may lack tact, it might also be true that you like to say it like it is. Unfortunately, many people can't take that. We've set up social constraints that don't allow it.

Nothing breaks down opportunity faster than the breakdown of communication. Too many people, and organizations, are remiss in communication. Your desire to share and hear well-intended, productive information cultivates positive energy.

Sure and authentic energy is refreshing. There's no polish, no pretense. Just *you*. If you are straightforward and blunt, you have the ability to tear away at social norms and constraints. Your genuine self can break through barriers and build a better conversation.

Creative, Innovative Energy

This energy is expansive and the source of most change in the world. It's the outside-the-box, no-limit thinking—and practical yet clever action—that can bust open the status quo, upset the applecart, and take chances for progress. Where would we be without those who had this energy? It can save the world, and it requires . . .

The Gifts of Imagination and Resourcefulness. It's not enough to just think differently; those thoughts must be executed. This energy requires an ability to be original and expansive in thinking while being grounded in follow-through.

If you are a romantic, you have the gift of hopes and dreams, and that means you have the seeds of energy for pursuing your ideals. The gift of imagination doesn't mean you have to create whole new worlds. If you've ever thought beyond tradition, initiated change, or shifted an accepted reality even a little bit, you have it.

You know that you are resourceful if you've ever met the challenge of getting through an unexpected situation; accomplished an overwhelming task when you had too little time; or juggled any number of people, places, and things at once. When you have a two-page to-do list for your work, home, and all the people and situations in your life, you need to be resourceful. This type of overloaded schedule is typical for most of us these days, in this world of *busy, but not productive.*

Taking your ideals and applying them, and combining them with the resourcefulness to execute, can give you that powerful creative, innovative energy.

Humble, Quiet Energy

The calm, certain, confident person can accomplish very big goals. Mother Teresa and Mahatma Gandhi were fierce leaders who engaged millions with this type of energy. It requires . . .

The Gifts of Principles and Gratitude. When you believe in very specific ideas, you have two choices: (1) you can be arrogant and self-righteous about them, spreading them loudly and frantically; or (2) you can find a resource in your faith, and know that if you keep moving forward, certain and confident in your ideals, others will feel the pull and draft off your energy.

Because this gift can be frustrating, it must be coupled with gratitude. By realizing that you've been given the gift of an idea to share, you can thank the powers that be for that gift and move forward in the humble, quiet energy of knowing that what you believe should be true, will be.

We all have the skill set to employ gratitude. What's great is that it is the gift that keeps on giving. It's an action that needs to be mobilized, a muscle that needs to be strengthened.

To get there, just be grateful and enjoy the fruits of that gift, as they are many.

Motivating, Inspiring, Contagious Energy

It's great to lead your life, but when you enroll a class, a team, an organization, a community, or the entire world to change for the better, you are a Leader with a capital L. True leaders do not do what they're not good at doing. When you have this energy, you might not even know you're moving others to change, and that's all right. It's wonderful to not even be aware that you're a model for others—it allows you to be their unsung hero, and that's a generous way to share your energy. This energy requires . . .

The Gifts of Caring and Nurturing. If you've ever taken someone under your wing and directed him or her away from distress and into satisfaction, then you have the ability to deploy a motivating, inspiring energy. It takes a green thumb to grow a fertile garden, and nurturing tendencies are excellent "fertilizer" for terrific teams. Great leaders manage each person with an understanding of who that person is and what he or she can be. The desire alone to help someone else grow is a great gift. If you're a natural "way to go!" supportive cheerleader, you can raise your game to lead others with an energy that sets the world on fire . . . you can be the flaming tornado.

∞

These are just a few examples of different types of energy and gifts. There are also external gifts given to us by life itself, which I cover in the next chapter.

One thing to look out for are the little *saboteurs* that disguise themselves as *external gifts.* For example, when you go to make a change, sometimes something will happen to dissuade or distract you. It happens when people are poised to quit their job and venture full-time into the business they've been "gestating." The week before they're ready to inform the company, they'll get a raise or a bonus. Don't let these false opportunities, these fake gifts, take you off course. That's the universe's way of testing you to see if you really want to achieve your dreams.

Unwrapping Your Gifts

In order to have the extreme energy that will propel you into a better life, you need to:

1. Find out just what your gifts are.

2. Not take them for granted.

3. Make them available.

4. Value them.

5. Not let them be overlooked by others.

At one of my seminars in California, a woman stood up to declare that she didn't have any gifts or skills.

"That's not possible," I said.

"I've never worked," she explained.

"What did you spend your life doing?"

"Raising my kids, and then helping raise my grandkids."

"How many kids and grandkids do you have?

"I've got six kids and 18 grandkids," she said.

I threw my hands up. "What? You just managed an army. Of course you have skill sets and dozens of gifts."

It is much easier to grow a company than it is to grow a human spirit—a responsible, soulful, amazing little person who contributes to society—as anyone who's done both knows. If you can raise a child, you can create a company. Those who raise a family have amazing gifts, yet many relegate themselves to "less than." Let me tell you this, great parents who've focused on their families could be CEOs of any company. Parents, guardians, aunts, uncles, grandparents . . . all have wonderful gifts that can be uncovered, reevaluated, and used to lead a new life.

It's sad to witness the many ways people undermine their potential. Somehow they just can't imagine they can be as great as they think they can be. I now know that it's an obligation to live life fully.

When I first started working for a well-known wealth builder, one of his colleagues, my direct boss, pulled me aside to tell me I was doing an excellent job. I noted that I was just supporting others and helping them do their jobs.

He shook his head, disappointed. "You keep tucking into the power of others, because you are scared of your own," he said.

That's a direct quote, and I'll never forget it. It drives me every day. You deserve to be great; and you need to tuck into *your own* power, be bigger, be better, be fantastic.

Your gifts have great value—don't throw or give them away. They are at the center of the *Energy Equation*. The power to be great is within you. Examine your inner strengths, your natural abilities, and everyday skills and use them to generate Yes! Energy.

One of our greatest gifts is the physical, sensual, free gift of just being alive, yet like so many of life's benefits, it is too often overlooked. . . .

CHAPTER 10

The Inquiry

What's the big game you're ready to play?

The Exercise

1. Consider the types of energy to which you aspire. List them in your journal.

2. What gifts do you have that service this energy? List them.

3. What services and support do you provide others that you take for granted or that aren't necessarily valued? How can you change that?

Next Steps:

Make a candid appraisal of your strengths, your skills, and your gifts. To help you be inclusive, consider how you make a living, not the job or title, but all of the actual skills you use. Look at the things you do every day that you might take for granted, but which you do very well and which come easily to you. Draw up as big of a list of your gifts as you can here. If you fall short, ask a trusted friend or relative for a few thoughts.

LEVERAGING
LIBIDO

The Drive of Nature

I love my libido. I know that might be embarrassing for some, but I live out loud, and state my truth. Although it has at times led me astray, for the most part it's been a great driving force in my life.

Most often identified with the sex drive, the libido is interpreted by psychologists to mean much more than that. They define *libido* as psychic energy and drive. It's a source of energy that comes from biological instinct. *Merriam-Webster's Collegiate Dictionary* says that libido is "derived from primitive biological urges" and "expressed in conscious activity." The online Wiktionary notes that libido connotes the desire to unite and bind with objects in the world. What a great perception of energy, the ability to *unite and bind*.

Some people think that the libido is the source of mind control, a variation on manifesting. I think it's more than coincidence that *libido* sounds a lot like the Latin *libertas,* which, of course, means "freedom."

Our instinctual biological energy is one of our greatest gifts. Yet too many people spend too much time suppressing their basic drive, their energy, and their power, allowing others to deem it dirty and dictate that it not be discussed. The very drive that can spiral a person into the virtuous cycle of the core vibration is then diminished. Despite years of progress and growth in most civilizations, too many societies revert to a constrained, Puritan repression, which is energy denying.

There's nothing more depleting to our energy than the suppression of our biological drive. We are given this gift at our core, yet we associate it with negative, primal, animal waywardness instead of what it can be: a directed, positive, life-engaging energy.

Yes, sex is part of libido, and sexual energy is exciting and fun. Yet I've also taken some major wrong turns because of sexual energy. In fact, one relationship choice I made, as I mentioned before, led me to compromise everything I built, everything I believed in, and too many people who believed in *me.* I take full responsibility for the choices I've made. My mistake, in this case, though, was letting one part of my life bleed into another. While this man brought excitement into my personal life, he brought values and a vision into my business that didn't resonate with mine or those of the rest of the organization. I almost let it take us down.

Letting Love in Through the Blind Side

I'd built a company through grit and grind, and created a community on which a lot of people depended and in which they were deeply involved. Then, because I live a fully integrated, no-walls life, I invited the personal into the professional with open arms. Unfortunately, my love was blind. I compromised my values and lost my way.

It's not super surprising that it happened. I'm a high-energy, engaged, sensual being, so when muscles, sparkling eyes, and a great smile approached, I fell. Unfortunately, everything else did, too.

It took me almost a decade to build and develop a renowned global company, and then I allowed someone in who almost broke it apart. This, of course, is not unusual. There are many men and women who build empires and allow a tug of the heart to enter the fortress and knock it apart. I learned a lot about myself and others. I also learned that although I'd led many things well, I needed to learn how to better lead my libido.

In the chapter "The Mystery of Sex Transmutation" from his book *Think and Grow Rich,* Napoleon Hill notes (in a time—the 1930s—when men were his target audience):

> Sex desire is the most powerful of human desires. When driven by this desire, men develop keenness of imagination, courage, will-power, persistence, and creative ability unknown to them at other times. So strong and impelling is the desire for sexual contact that men freely run the risk of life and reputation to indulge it. When harnessed, and redirected along other lines, this motivating force maintains all of its attributes of keenness of imagination, courage, etc., which may be used as powerful creative forces in literature, art, or in any other profession or calling, including, of course, the accumulation of riches.

Why this chapter isn't spread and read by everyone in the world, I don't know. It says that we have a button, installed at birth, that can be pushed for energy, optimism, excitement, and freedom. How great is that? A vital key to ∞EOE∞ is our gift of libido.

Hill goes on to say:

> Destroy the sex glands, whether in man or beast, and you have removed the major source of action. For proof of this, observe what happens to any animal after it has been castrated. A bull becomes as docile as a cow after it has been altered sexually. Sex alteration takes out of the male, whether man or beast, all the fight that was in him. Sex alteration of the female has the same effect.

Placing a Premium on Primal Ambition, Action, and Sales

Much like hunger motivates so much more than a desire to eat, our biological drives affect our actions in many areas of our lives. Psychiatrist Carl Jung defined libido as creative, psychic energy that helps us develop and discover our true self. Neurologist and psychoanalyst Sigmund Freud, who popularized the term, said libido was a force of instinct.

I associate libido with ambition, the capacity to act, and the desire to interact. Libido reigns over much of our ability to socialize and exchange. It also spurs on much of our energy and optimism. Without it, life is dull, inwardly directed, and smaller. Channeled and managed with goodwill and respect toward others, the libido is a powerful force. It's a wonderful gift to celebrate.

Most successful athletes, artists, politicians, professionals, and entrepreneurs have ambition that comes from an action-oriented, competitive, driving nature associated with libido. I'm certain that my early training and continued involvement in both sports and music, on teams and in community, help me funnel and direct the assets of libido to support business success.

Successful entrepreneurs usually have healthy libidos in that they have a tremendous ability to lead, motivate, and enroll others. In business exchanges, they are excellent at uniting and bonding. The energy of an effective entrepreneur, in sales and marketing, is not pushing . . . it's not dominating. It's *serving*.

Sales is an exchange of energy. It's an understanding, a reading of psychic wants and needs. In other words, it's a well-tuned libido. A healthy libido is tied in directly to one's knowing core: confidence and certainty. It's not arrogant or overwhelming; but rather, it's calm, easy, and engaging. Good salespeople know that what they have is going to serve, so they are more focused on others than on themselves. In fact, in our organization, we shift the word from *sales* to *service,* which pivots the effort from self-interest to outward engagement.

Too often in business, people get weird about sales. This feeling is all internal, coming only from themselves and their own deservability. Think about it. As a salesperson, you're providing supply for demand. You're no different from the barista on the other side of the coffee stand or the attendant at the gas station. Those sales folks don't get all weird about selling their goods and services—because they're not negotiating. They have what the customer needs, and the customer comes to them to get it.

If you're in a business that is in line with your values, then you know you're selling something that you can serve to others with certainty. *Sales* has a slimy connotation because so many people don't care about what they're selling. If you're leading a business or an organization and you feel like you don't know what you're talking about, that's a problem. You've got to create a living for yourself from a place of certainty. Then you can use your gift of libido and energy to build your business or do well in your career.

If you ever want to see an excellent use of the gift of libido, go be sold to. Go to a car dealership, an insurance company, or a commission retail store, and ask for the leading salesperson. Watch that person's style, approach, initial engagement, and powerful closing statements ("I'll just wrap that up for you") or questions ("Would you like a doughnut with your coffee?"). Notice the individual's skills, rapport, how many questions he or she asks, *what* is asked, and when and how.

Next time you go into a clothing store, notice that the worst salespeople pounce on you as soon as you walk in. The best observe you, watch where you go, what you're looking at, and what you're avoiding. At a certain point they engage you with the attitude of "How can I make your experience better?"

In this example, if you see the parallel between successful salespeople and those on the dating scene, you're becoming aware of the pervasiveness of libido in social interaction.

Life's Free Gifts

Libido commits us to engage, make exchanges with, and in many situations, serve others. This primal gift is one of the many we're given to nurture and cultivate. Life offers myriad free gifts to celebrate. Speak with anyone who can't eat or sleep and that person will tell you right off the bat what a gift these things are.

I have many appetites, urges, and drives. I feed and protect these gifts because they are the essence of living. They are, in fact, vitality itself. Unfortunately, many of us are just trying to get by. We eat quickly, schedule sex, and sleep a few hours here and there, while noisy, unproductive thoughts roil in our brains, making us restless. We may work out or squeeze in some exercise, but we don't connect it to the gift of physicality and the joy of movement, honoring the body itself.

We depend on our libidos to help feed our energy and drive, our attitude and optimism. In turn, our libidos need the great gifts of life as sources of nourishment. Fortunately, there are many:

— **The gift of water.** They say 75 percent of the earth (and our bodies) is made up of water. In too few places is pure water free and available. In many parts of the world, though, the investment in a good filter makes it both. Water is a fantastic source of energy. It keeps the organs hydrated, the nutrients flowing, and the brain keen and awake. I'm also a big fan of swimming and floating about in the ocean, lakes, and rivers whenever possible. It's energizing to immerse oneself in the life-giving particles of these bodies of water.

— **The gifts of food and drink.** It's not new news to announce that proper nutrition can increase your energy . . . but food and drink are not *just* sources of nutrients.

We've lost so much pleasure that can be derived from food—growing, preparing, and sharing it. Those who have a garden can tell you the restorative nature of tending to their own herbs, fruits, and vegetables. Consider the difference between having one person cook for several others or each for themselves, versus the idea of gathering family or friends in the kitchen and socializing over the cutting, dicing, and chopping. Picking up fast food can't begin to compare to breaking bread with others and enjoying their companionship.

A Latin teacher told me that the word *company* means "to share (*co-*) bread (*pan*) with." You can't really have true company without a little food passed back and forth.

Moderation is a gift, too. As I've touched upon, the whole idea of depriving oneself of this and that is a major energy and attitude drain. There are so many great ways to feed our appetites. Learning to appreciate, and educate ourselves on, what different foods and beverages have to offer allows us to tap into whole new avenues of positive energy.

— The gifts of physical activity and stamina. I like to ski, run, bike, and hike. I'm very grateful for my physical stamina. Good genes are a gift. My father came from hearty German stock. My mother has Swedish and German ancestry. My parents were always strong and able, and I feel very fortunate to have a body on which I can rely. When I feel good in my body, I have more energy and a better attitude.

— The gift of the great outdoors. This world is, in the truest sense of the word, *awesome*. Yet it seems too many of us are spending more time indoors, watching TV, playing video games, or surfing the Internet. When was the last time you went for a walk in the woods, dipped your toe in a river, felt sand under your feet, or rested your hand on the smooth and warm face of a rock? Sounds pretty nice, right?

There are huge vibrations of energy that come from the earth. Few things can shift you into a fresh state of hope like sunlight on your face or the sound of gentle rain bouncing through tree branches. Get out there and get some free energy.

— The gifts of travel and culture. We have some really fun people in my community who like to explore the world. They plan trips around the globe for adventure, culture, and education. To spend a lifetime in one place with one group of people is playing small. There are so many individuals to learn from and cultures to which you can expose yourself. Even if it means getting in the car and driving a hundred miles to a small town just to see something different, do it. Travel experiences can shift your perceptions, change your thinking, get you in a new conversation, and enhance your energy.

— **The gifts of education and new experiences.** Learning infuses energy. New experiences and information perk up the brain and foster growth. There is no reason, ever, to be bored. Get out and engage. Try something new.

This is age-old advice, yet too few venture beyond the comfortable. Your comfort is your constraint. Raise the bar when it comes to your own expectations and make an effort, at least once a month, to try something new. Education and experience support the gifts of change, perception, and growth . . . and help us better ourselves.

— **The gift of other people.** This is life's greatest gift of all. One of my favorite and best sources of energy is conversation. I meet thousands of men and women every year, and with each exchange, I gain something new. It's detrimental to our positive energy to close ourselves off to others. It's a sad world when we act out of fear and distrust, disliking others before we've even engaged with them. The less we hold preconceptions and judgment, and the more we embrace open-minded, healthy, "goodwill" libido, the better off everyone will be.

When we expect the best of others, we create the best of ourselves. While many educators and motivational speakers talk about their "clients," our team at Live Out Loud calls it a *community*. We enroll people to be a part of an inclusive and expansive supportive, helpful, interactive, high-energy community in a rich conversation.

Loving Your Libido

Look at all the gifts you get for free just for playing the game of being a human being. We have appetites and drives and libido . . . and the gifts of food, drink, water, travel, culture, fitness, sleep, meditation, prayer, and health. We can educate ourselves and gain experiences. We can attract and engage other people. We can walk in the world and breathe in the fresh, energizing air.

Life is glorious. It's yours for the taking, but *you* must take it. You must give and share, act and engage. You must commit to and lead a life of gratitude. Indulge in life's gifts . . . they will enhance your own. There's no time to worry about living exactly right. You can't be perfect, so don't waste time and deplete energy trying to be. Get into action and get going. . . .

CHAPTER 11

The Inquiry:

At the most basic, primal level, what gifts do you appreciate and enjoy? How do these support your energy and optimism?

The Exercise:

1. Think about your health. Are you taking good care of yourself physically, spiritually, *and* mentally? What steps are you taking to promote that in each of these three areas?

2. List the gifts of life that feed your energy best.

3. Write down life's gifts that you could engage with/in more.

Next Steps:

Go outside and take a walk, during which you consider all the great gifts that are freely available to you. How can you use them to increase your energy, and shift into or preserve a positive attitude?

THE
PROBLEM
WITH PERFECT

And the Power of Imperfection

Many people would rather do nothing than fail or make a mistake. They're so afraid of how they're perceived that they'd rather deny their gifts altogether. Gifts, though, are not unassailable. They need to be recognized, nurtured, and protected. Yet they are vulnerable to attack. One of the most vicious threats, deep at the core of people's failure to properly exploit their God-given gifts, is a toxic little offender called . . . *perfection*. Yes, that's right, there's a problem with perfect.

Here's the news flash if you don't know it already: Perfect doesn't exist. There are no perfect people; there is no perfect world, no perfect place. While with the right energy and attitude, we can perceive *everything* to be perfect, trying to attain or achieve that state is a painful pursuit.

Perfect is an ideal created by some sadist to prompt mere mortals to chase a concept with no end in sight. In fact, there are many religions that teach that perfection is beyond the human realm, an achievement for God alone. It is, in effect, arrogant—an affront to God—to attempt to be perfect. Yet, over and over again, humans have perfection as a goal: "I strive to be perfect," "Practice makes perfect," "Perfect is as perfect does," and so on.

Perfection is *what?* It's a pain in the butt is what it is, and the pursuit of it has stopped one too many potential success stories from ever getting written. That stinks.

An acquaintance once explained to me that his parents always told him how great and wonderful he was, and it paralyzed him because he never wanted to try something new and prove them wrong. He grew up fearful and playing small, even though he was smart, talented, and able. It wasn't so much his parents' expectations, but the implication that he was already as great as he could be, so why be less than perfect by actually doing anything?

One of the many problems with "perfect" is that it doesn't allow for fast action or significant growth. I appreciate my gift to be in action. I use my energy to create. That creation *generates* my energy. Part of the expense of doing business is the cost of wrong turns and mistakes. If a business or a person isn't willing to make mistakes and learn from those mistakes, there is no growth. Of course, I try to preserve my energy by learning from the mistakes and imperfections of those who came before me. That's why I've had mentors and coaches since I was 17, to help me cut to the chase of some of these lessons.

You should always have a mentor or coach in your life. As George Leonard says in his wonderful book *Mastery: The Keys to Success and Long-Term Fulfillment,* "The courage of a master is measured by his or her willingness to surrender." I believe in surrendering to a coach or teacher and letting that individual show me the way, instead of pursuing the route I think perfect for me.

I constantly try to change and grow. As those who've worked with me know, this means I try many different things. Several don't work, but more do. The gift of being in action keeps me from worrying too much about stumbling. If I falter, I get up, fix the problem, and learn from it. More and more, I make fewer and fewer mistakes, but I needed those initial ones to learn anything in the first place.

Perfectionists do not like surrendering or making mistakes. They don't like failing, because that's not perfect, or good enough, and they were conditioned to be so. In these cases, obstacles are avoided or denied, rather than confronted. Since every path to anything worthwhile has obstacles, perfectionists do not pursue these paths. They'd rather, like my acquaintance mentioned earlier in the chapter, do nothing. In fact, by doing nothing, they can imagine that had they tried, they might have succeeded.

Too many live in this place of dreaming of success rather than taking a chance and seeing if it's possible. Worse, many do take a chance, fail, and crawl right back into the small place from which they came. It takes many failures to succeed, so dipping one's toes into action doesn't work. You have to dive all the way in and swim imperfectly to success.

This stasis, this nonmovement, is inaction. If action creates growth, then *in*action shrinks a life. The next thing you know, your life is small. That is dangerous. Those in a mentality of "Take cover" go nowhere. Acting this way, or surrounding yourself with those who have this attitude, depletes energy.

Action is a gift. We are here to do and create. If we were meant to sit around and just be, to just exist, then we wouldn't have been given the gifts of intelligence and physicality . . . ambition and desire. Our biological drives create "want." Those wants spur action that pushes us to do and grow. Fear of failure is kryptonite to energy and optimism.

In too many pursuits, people get tangled up in business that's not productive. While perfectionists will run around trying to do every task as perfectly as possible, those who lead lives of abundance and fulfillment focus on their gifts of action and execution and cultivate an ability to perceive perfection even when everything's not quite perfect.

A good place to begin to embrace imperfection is physically. Consider your own body. Instead of wasting energy focused on the skin that's not glowing, the shape that's not shapely, or the hair that's receding, consider instead how wonderful your physical being is. I've seen women who have several kids and then lament the stretched skin and loss of taut muscles. Are you kidding me? You had kids. Get over it. That's your body. The celebrity pictures on magazines are airbrushed and doctored. No one, not even the prettiest model, is perfect. Humans are *im*perfect, and imperfection is human.

The Fight Is On: Gifts vs. Saboteurs

The problem with perfection is that it also makes our gifts vulnerable to the attacks of outside and internal forces. Fortunately, we have *other* gifts to protect against these acts of sabotage.

External Forces

Outside forces that attack our gifts include *criticism, judgment, rejection,* and the black hole of *indifference.* All of which can squelch the brightest talents.

— The gift of *learning* vs. the saboteur of *criticism.* It's painful to be scolded and corrected. Yet the ability to take criticism well is a gift. The ability to *offer* it well, to do so constructively, is also a gift. In order to exploit our energy to the fullest, we must value and appreciate who we are and the gifts we've been given. Obviously, though, we can't go through life thinking we're God's gift to the world. Fortunately, part of our process of growing and progressing along our path involves the gift of learning.

The ability to learn is one of our greatest skills. Babies do it from the get-go. As they're constructively criticized, they learn what's helpful to them in living a life and what's not. If they're scolded in such a way that is traumatic, though, the lesson is less productive, and the gift of learning damaged. This goes on throughout a lifetime.

In order to continue to learn in a way that fuels our energy and builds an optimistic attitude, we must be able to absorb good criticism and deflect the hurtful and mean critics. In turn, we must also work on our own ability to criticize constructively. I've found it helpful to begin with an acknowledgment or positive comment. This is a good approach to management and leadership. One good rule—sometimes challenging, but worth attempting—is the 5:1 ratio, or five positive comments for every one criticism. Additionally, I try to focus on the behavior or the action, not the person or his or her character. Mostly, when in critic mode, I make sure my goal is always to stay away from *hurtful* and get to *helpful*.

— **The gift of *tolerance* vs. the saboteur of *judgment*.** As I mentioned earlier, I'm not above the judgment that comes at me. I know about it. I read about it. I've had horrible things said about me. Years ago when I decided to put myself out for public viewing, so to speak, I made the decision to be judged. That doesn't mean I have to accept it. I do, though, have to listen to some judgment around me, and evaluate the truth of it, because that's what helps me learn and grow.

We must use our gift of tolerance, for ourselves and others. I make it a rule to focus on the judgment from people who know me. If my close friends share an opinion about a choice I've made, I listen to it. First, I consider the context of the situation. Is it one in which a friend's judgment might be more objective and clear than my own? Second, I think about the other person's perspective and try to understand if the judgment comes from an objective place. Is the observation infused with too much of my friend's own experiences and biases, or is he or she providing clearheaded counsel? Third, I decide how important it is for me to take on his or her judgment.

A big problem for many is that our affection for friends, partners, and family blinds us to their judgment. If you grew up in a codependent, dysfunctional family but don't even recognize that fact, then you're going to accept a lot of negative judgment that will deplete your energy and make *you* negative. Opening up your world to healthy people and enlightening experiences helps you find better sources of growth.

Similarly, I try to keep a constant check on being judgmental. Sometimes, of course, I can't help it. If someone walks by with an ugly hat on, I have to work hard not to have thoughts that don't suit my values. But most of the time, I think about my thinking and work against intolerance. Being curious and asking questions, instead of jumping to conclusions, seems to help a lot.

When I am judgmental (and I'm lucky enough to know I'm being that way), I admit it, which helps me, too. For instance, there is one area in which I know I'm judgmental—and those are instances when I observe people saying one thing and then doing another. That's one of my biggest pet peeves. While I try to be tolerant of those who operate in this way, I'm judgmental of that type of process. And I say so. For the most part, though, I find that while I can be constructive in my criticism, my judgment is usually not helpful. The best thing I can do is stay tolerant and focus on gifts—mine and those of others.

— **The gift of *fortitude* vs. the saboteur of *rejection*.** Getting rejected depletes energy. We must shield ourselves from the negative energy that is, in fact, not ours. It's exhausting to work hard toward a goal only to be pushed backward. Entrepreneurs deal with this often. Few new ideas have surged forward without rejection. Hearing *no* is part of the process of getting to *Yes!*

Fortunately, you have the gift of fortitude. It feels bad to be rejected in one's personal or work life. All of it *feels* personal, but that feeling can be shifted with the right perspective. If you go out there and attempt to collect the *no*'s in order to get to the *Yes!* then you make rejection part of the process. You don't go out and expect rejection—that's defeatist—but when it happens, you accept rejection and move forward.

It's vital for anyone who wants to live a life of ∞EOE∞ not to allow rejection to kill a gift. Too many have given up too soon because they failed and threw in the towel. Abraham Lincoln lost several elections before he became President. Henry Ford was constantly directed back out the door when he pitched his ideas. The myth of the rust-prevention solvent and degreaser WD-40 is that it is so named because that was the number of attempts it took to find a formula that finally achieved the desired effect of water displacement.

Everyone experiences rejection. The shame of it is if that rejection then allows you to reject your own gifts.

— **The gifts of *faith* and *certainty* vs. the saboteur of *indifference*.** Some might say that indifference is the cruelest attack on one's gifts. While criticism, judgment, and rejection are hurtful, they are at least active, if negative, acknowledgments of one's gifts. Indifference can trigger a variation on the proverbial philosophical inquiry: if a gift falls in the forest and no one hears it, is it a gift?

Indifference, though, is not reality. It can't be reality for those who live in extreme energy. It just means that the gifts are being displayed in the wrong arena—pearls before swine, as they say. The gifts of faith and certainty help us stay optimistic and energized.

When we truly recognize our gifts, we realize that these are, in the true sense of the word, *gifts*. They're not skills we created, but rather talents we were given and with which we were entrusted. Naturally, that leads to faith, and faith pushes certainty. If we truly believe in our missions and motives and we are celebrating our gifts by using them, then no amount of indifference can get in our way.

Internal Forces

Adversaries from within that can attack our gifts include *fear, guilt, shame, embarrassment,* and *small thinking.* All of these can do damage. . . .

— **The gift of *courage* vs. the saboteur of *fear*.** Fear is the biggest saboteur out there. What are we all so afraid of? Failure?

Rejection? Trying, perhaps? Maybe we fear wasted effort or potential disappointment.

Think about it, though. You may not be afraid of failing. You might be afraid of the enormous responsibility of success. Even if you don't succeed, or at least don't succeed in the way you wanted, you still did *something*. That experience of making an effort will make the next effort that much easier. If you spent yesterday stuck in your old story, but today you decided to stop holding on to that unproductive thesis and change the conversation, that's progress. As Les Brown says in his book *Live Your Dreams*, "There comes a time when you have to drop your burdens in order to fight for yourself and your dreams." Drop your burdens. Yes. That's it. If you drop your burdens, if you change the conversation to a new story, that's progress, and that progress may lead to success. Plans rarely go exactly as you think they will, and success may not look the way you thought it would, but forward motion always puts you a step ahead of where you were.

The gift of courage can support you against fear.

There's an old saying: "Burn your boats." It refers to a battle cry, long ago when sailors disembarked from their ship to attack on land only to hear from behind them their naval commander order: "Burn the boats." Retreat no longer an option, the troops were committed to the task at hand. Gifts need your similar commitment, so burn your boats.

I'm always telling my clients: if nothing else, get in *action*. On our team, in my community, we see ourselves on track for greater things all the time. In fact, we create so much exponential activity and move so fast that we often have to recalculate normal activity into "Live Out Loud Years." We do in one year what most do in three. When our train starts moving too fast for some, we tell them, "Hold on—stay focused."

The key is to get in spiritual shape and stay in motion. Many of us have atrophied little spiritual and "action" muscles that need to be reconditioned. I'm constantly told to slow down. My response, of course, is that others should speed up. If my speed intimidates them, I can't slow down to make them feel good.

If you are fully exploiting your gifts, doing all you're capable of, and blasting into extreme energy, you can stay on the train. Usually, it's those last few troubling obstacles that represent the storm before the calm. Yet that's where many quit. If you're on track to reach your goal, then it doesn't matter if you're getting queasy or uncomfortable. You have support, you have a team, you can handle the speed and stay in the game. You'll get stronger, and better—and your gifts will grow.

— **The gift of** *confidence* **vs. the saboteurs of** *guilt, shame,* **and** *embarrassment.* We feel selfish or unjustified in recognizing our gifts, so we play small.

Let's face it, though—you can't help anyone else until you've helped yourself, and if you're constrained or struggling in any way, then you don't have the freedom and energy to help others. By owning your gifts, you empower yourself to create abundance for yourself and those you love. As I've mentioned before, playing small is bad for you and those around you; it serves nothing and no one. When people engage scarcity thinking and believe that there is not enough, they fight and compete, and create fear and anxiety. If only you understood that there is more than enough for everyone, you would go get it with abandon. Abundance creates abundance.

Opportunity is not a numbers game; it's about finding the right thing at the right time. Those who fight over the same piece of pie, instead of trying to make the pie bigger for everyone, do no one any good and dishonor themselves.

The gift of confidence, in truly believing in yourself and your gifts, can overcome guilt, shame, and embarrassment. Trust yourself and your abilities. This will inspire and uplift others.

— **The gift of** *unlimited human potential* **vs. the saboteur of** *small thinking.* If you're conditioned by negative criticism and harsh judgment, you may grow up thinking small and playing to lose. As with external criticism and judgment, our internal criticism and judgment can attack our gifts and be a detriment to our energy and optimism. These internal messages allow us to think that we're not good enough. Not good enough to accomplish more than the average person, not good enough to stand out from the crowd, not good enough to lead, and not even good enough to have a life that goes beyond basic survival. That's painful thinking.

There are many models of excellence and abundance out there, and you can learn from, and *become,* one of them. Even these lives don't exemplify perfection, because there's no such thing. Life can be great without being perfect. There's every reason to believe that you can have a life as fabulous as the one you perceive someone else is having, without getting it exactly right (whatever that means).

The gift of unlimited human potential is yours as much as it is anyone else's. There was an idea, once upon a time, that life could be more than hunting and gathering and protecting and defending. There was an idea, in history, that humans could explore other lands and other planets. There was an idea, more recently, that people could communicate immediately and constantly without being in each other's presence. These were ideas of big thinking, and they all became reality.

There's absolutely no logical reason humans needed to grow past our basic instincts and primitive living. People could have remained "contained" in their early ways. Yet we didn't. Ambitions, desire, hunger, and drive propelled us through evolutions and revolutions to the places we are now.

As individuals, we need to continue to progress and grow. Or else we risk getting smaller and possibly moving backward to a place of less ease and comfort, and more fear and despair. Small thinking squelches the best of what it is to be a person on this planet.

The gift of unlimited human potential must be nourished in order to attack small thinking. It begins with changing the conversation. If you wonder why, then *ask* why. Don't let something be just because it's always been. Too many people seek permission, follow others, and let tradition and "the way it's always been" dictate their lives. Those who live their gifts exploit their gifts. They make things happen. They think big and without limits. When you get a progressive, exciting, energizing idea in your head, consider how that new thought got delivered into your head in the first place. Those thoughts and ideas may be gifts. It's your duty to celebrate and exploit them.

Combined with the rest of the *Energy Equation*, especially the ideas of getting support through the proper *team* and executing the right steps at the right times with productive *sequencing*, our gifts can take us to wherever we want to go.

Preserving Perceived Perfection— a Macroeconomic Crisis

I stated in my letter at the front of this book that while it's important to manage debt and risk, we don't have to live in scarcity, saving, and fear. We can have abundant, fun lives that are lived responsibly. That concept is the new conversation, and it begins by shifting our view of our place in this world.

We grew up in an industrial-age conversation that began over a century ago. Prior to that, the entrepreneurship of innovators, inventors, and dreamers built great nations. Somehow, though, the most recent conversation locked into the dated idea that you *receive* an education, *have* a job, *work* hard, and *plan* to retire.

Yuck, yuck, yuck, and yuck. By doing this, we become mindless, preserving what we see as perfect, when in fact it's anything but. If we want a better world, we must uncover and use our gifts. We can't find our laurels if we're just resting on them.

— **First** of all, education cannot be passive. Children shouldn't "receive" anything. They should dig in actively and *take* their education. We all know that lectures are passive, and that question-and-answer dialogue is active. We all know that sitting still and listening is boring, and movement and interaction are energizing. We all know that while theory and academic discussions are interesting and necessary for change, action and experiences lead to real knowledge. Yet—our schools remain as they've ever been: institutions of learning, instead of incubators of talents and gifts.

I'd like to see a change in that conversation. Even the word *institution* is cold and stale. Let's up the education ante by changing the system, helping children think creatively and expansively, tapping into all their skills, using even their latent and unique gifts. I'm working now with a college to change their entire finance and business syllabus. In my world, education is about growth, and building. We do not sit in comfort, thinking that things are perfect. We get uncomfortable and don't mind imperfection in pursuit of positive, healthy change.

— **Second** of all, there's too much focus on *jobs*. The expectation of most people in this world is that they will go out and get a job, that they deserve a job, that they have to have a job. That's a slave mentality that tricks us into thinking everything is fine—perfect, in fact. It certainly doesn't encourage people to use their God-given talents and gifts. What built the United States and other great pioneering, developed, democratic countries is the entrepreneurial spirit to create. If everyone just went out and got a job, then we'd have one factory or mill for which we all would work forever and ever. This builds nothing.

Fortunately, thanks to our freedom, our rights, and our liberties, no one has to buy into the economy and community into which they're born. Throughout history, people have created their own microeconomies where they find their talents and gifts, and then they've traded and leveraged those skills, as well as their resources.

In my community of entrepreneurs, we do exactly that. People dig into their gifts and engage in a market of exchange for those gifts, creating businesses to supply and support each other. Its setup is similar to how villages functioned centuries ago. And similar to how contemporary corporations were built. Ray Kroc didn't just build McDonald's. He used his gifts and talents to build a channel of supply and demand that enabled farmers, warehouses, distributors, transport companies, paper and packaging companies, marketers, and various other manufacturers and service professionals to develop and grow businesses. Fortunately, Ray Kroc didn't think things were perfect. He was willing to take a risk for change and improvement.

Interdependent entrepreneurs abound. It's a party into which anyone can invite themselves. It requires recognizing that everything is not perfect. It requires seeing a demand and creating a supply, filling a niche or a void, or empowering a chain by providing a stronger link. This perspective of the economy and community changes the conversation and allows individuals to use their gifts.

If you wait for the perfect opportunity for your perfect self, though, you will be waiting a very long time.

— **Third**, working hard and making a lot of money is an illusory correlation. There are plenty of people who've worked hard and gotten nowhere. Similarly, there are those who have great wealth and didn't break their backs. I'm not saying wealth building is easy. It certainly is not. There's no way you can sit on your couch eating bonbons and become a millionaire. Lazy is lazy—it gets you nowhere. But working hard just to work hard is not smart. There is a difference between busy and productive. Those who know their gifts and use their strengths do not have to work as hard as those who depend on others and do the work they're told rather than the work at which they excel. Similarly, those who employ the 80-20 rule, who know that good enough is sometimes good enough, can enjoy and realize more than perfectionists.

— **Fourth**, planning to retire is planning to die. Retirement cannot be the endgame. In my conversation, the goal is Freedom Day—that time in your life when you can do what you want, when and with whom you want. Because you *can*. This doesn't mean stopping everything you ever did. If you like the way you make money, you should make money until the day you die. Unfortunately, if you have a job, it's less likely that that will appeal to you.

The new conversation in Yes! Energy is to dream a goal that's appealing. Sitting in your slippers in front of the television is not a dream. Well, okay . . . it may be for some. But a few days or weeks of that and you're going to get bored. Not to mention bedsores. If you learn to educate yourself in a new and exciting way, you're going to want to learn your entire life. If you let go of a job and the old conversation of working hard, your work will excite and propel you, and you'll want to work the rest of your life.

Freedom Day excites and energizes. While retirement implies that stage of life before death, Freedom Days can occur early and often. They are big stimulating goals of how you want your life to look at various stages. I reached my first big financial goal before I was 34, and attained my Freedom Day shortly thereafter. Because I like to work, I've had to readjust my goals, and my endgame, because the reality is, there is no endgame. A life of extreme optimism and energy requires having fun over and over and over again.

Be Less-Than to Get More-Than

There are so many areas in which we fail to live up to our gifts because we are afraid of being less than perfect. For example, most of us don't want to . . .

— **Be wrong.** If you're going to try to do a lot in this life, you're going to be wrong sometimes. In order to even attempt to change the conversation, you're going to have to allow yourself to try out new ideas and thoughts. Sometimes these concepts will prove incorrect. When I have a new idea, I reach out to my community to debate and discuss it. This means I have to be open to being wrong. Opening up a dialogue only to rationalize, defend, or justify closes down the avenues to growth.

— **Look stupid.** There are times you're going to look stupid. Spend one day with a child under four and no doubt you will be asked to do, or be told you've done, something that's just plain stupid, probably by the child himself. When you collect experiences that create the evidence you need in order to be confident, you're going to look stupid sometimes. Being vulnerable to saying and doing stupid things helps you strengthen your gifts. It builds your lightness, your humility, your candor, and your empathy. The best gift, in these cases, is your *sense of humor.* Believe me, that's why mine's so good.

— **Keep falling.** I'm an expert skier who learned through lessons and commitment. I was willing to continue falling. Even when I hit a level approaching "advanced," which is certainly respectable, and quite comfortable, I kept going. Eager to experience more and more of a mountain, I needed to up my game. Which meant falling. And so what? I'd have a tag sale of equipment, and a wardrobe strewn over the mountain. Who cares? I'd get that run the next time.

Life can be so much bigger and better if you're willing to let go of "perfect." Allow perfect to be perception, not reality, and every day of your life will be a happy one. *Let go* of perfect and you will *let in* a lot more excitement, energy, and optimism than you ever thought possible. This will attract others, and soon you'll be part of a whole new team. . . .

∞EOE∞

CHAPTER 12

The Inquiry:

How has the pursuit of perfection gotten in your way?

The Exercise:

1. Consider what you perceive to be your greatest failure and what you learned from your mistakes.

2. Examine the external and internal saboteurs that threaten your gifts.

3. Reflect on something you would like to try but are afraid of not doing well. Write down what, if anything, is stopping you from going out and attempting this pursuit.

Next Steps:

What's your Freedom Day? Write out what it would look like. Who is there? Where is it? What are you doing? This visual should be in your head as you move forward, imperfectly, to uncover and exploit your gifts.

∞ E O E ∞

Part IV: Honoring Gifts
Summary Inquiry

1.   What gifts might you be ignoring, using for small and mean-
     ingless purposes, or giving away?

2.   List your skills, talents, and gifts. Don't be modest.

3.   Consider the gifts of those you admire, and write down the
     talents and skills they have to which you can aspire.

4.   Which of life's free gifts do you take full advantage of? Which
     of life's free gifts already help you increase your energy and
     improve your attitude? Which would you like to better ex-
     ploit?

5.   What might be sabotaging your gifts?

6.   How can you get things done faster to preserve and fuel your
     energy without getting in your own way?

PART V

TEAM AND SEQUENCING

$$\{\Delta C+[F(2C)*D]+G+T\}S=\infty EOE\infty$$

"Leadership should
be born out of the
understanding of the needs
of those who would
be affected by it."

— **MARIAN ANDERSON**, SINGER
AND CIVIL-RIGHTS LEADER

THE
POWER
OF TEAM

Support and Community
Every Day, Everywhere

When you grow up in a small town, you realize five things very quickly:

1. You don't have every talent and skill you need in order to do well, or even survive.

2. Few do.

3. Even those individuals who (seem to) know how to do everything don't have enough time to do it.

4. If folks work together, gifts and time can complement each other, and the whole can be much stronger than the sum of its parts.

5. By working in teams, you learn how to teach people how to treat you and how to treat others with respect.

In my town, we had to team up if we wanted to get anything done, so I learned about teamwork early on. Since there weren't that many kids in my school, if we wanted to have a basketball team, everyone had to join, even if some weren't good at it. Similarly, if we wanted to put on a play, every kid had to take part in the drama club so we could get the show on the stage. That's why I played softball—so the softball players could play their sport, and so that, in turn, I could be out there excelling in basketball with the softball players who'd joined to make a full team. I played five instruments, several being needed in orchestra and band, but only a few of which I was actually good at; and I was in choir, although I couldn't sing a note. Talk about imperfection.

All of this allowed me to learn early on the benefits of teamwork and community, of combining gifts and energies.

The Costs and Benefits

Before I even begin this chapter, I want to address an issue that comes up often when I talk or write about *team:* the cost. Many people think that it's cost prohibitive to engage and enroll others to help them with their tasks. These people do not understand that a team, the *right* team, pays for itself over and over.

They say that time is money. The best way to *get time* is to *have team.* When we teach people in our Live Out Loud Community how to make cash fast, we emphasize the importance of generating immediate sales and gathering immediate support. That upfront money needs to be spent to buy time before it buys anything else. Time is bought through team.

Those who say they can't afford a team don't understand the value of time in their pursuit of their ventures. If you generate $100 immediately, and then use that cash to pay someone to clean your house every week, you just gave yourself those hours you used to spend cleaning to go generate more cash. Small-business owners who are great at strategy and marketing, but spend their time building a website because they don't want to hire someone to do that, are wasting countless hours doing something they are not good at doing and which someone else could do better and faster. Instead, they could hire an expert, spend their time selling, and generate more cash.

The team does not have to be big to start. The building of one, though, person by person, needs to be immediate.

In fact, the first team I was ever on was the family farm. Historically, farm families had a lot of children to help out with the physical labor. Mine was no exception. From as far back as I can remember, my siblings and I were asked to help out. Although it was a lot of hard work, early mornings, and constant chores, looking back I was proud of the work we did and felt good being in on the effort. At home, in school, and in my town, I enjoyed this reciprocity—others helping me, me helping them.

When I left my hometown, it surprised me to find that this was not the norm. I was disappointed. It was every man for himself. That made no sense to me. If someone had a skill set, chances were that I had a complementary one, so why compete? Why not work together, pool our talents, and build something bigger and better?

There is abundance out there, if you just go get it. It is way easier to find a team and create opportunities than most people think. Once you start to see how to locate opportunities, you will not *stop* seeing them.

One of my colleagues had a brother who did landscaping. His business did okay; he was getting by. One summer she had her deck built. The deck builder's business wasn't going very well at all. She approached him and offered to have her brother put his phone number on his truck. In exchange, the deck builder would refer all of *his* customers to her brother. A classic joint venture. As a result, both of their businesses grew. Not one to give away her value, my colleague took a nice cut from both sides. Now, she often coordinates referrals and joint ventures and has made quite a nice business for herself, using her gifts of relationship and team building.

Doing Less, Making More . . . Through Team

I accomplish all I do because of team. When people tell me they don't have time, I know they need *team*. Teams are time, teams are energy, teams are attitude.

I'm constantly enrolling others. If I see someone with a talent that can help me get to my goal, I do what I can to get that person on a project or venture with me. For many, it's uncomfortable to ask for help. (Just talk to that half of the population who won't even stop to get directions!) There are also those who find it very difficult to receive help. Both asking and receiving make some of us uncomfortable.

While it's easy to stay in a nonthreatening, quiet place, that's numbing. If you're not uncomfortable, you haven't pushed yourself enough to stretch. By asking for help, by allowing others to work with you and you with others, you can grow. Growing and becoming bigger than you ever thought you could be is energizing and exciting.

I have teams everywhere: in my business, for each project I do, at home. I'm constantly supported. Why not? I've heard others judge me for having help at home, as if to imply that I'm not with my kids. They should only know how amazing and supportive my home team is. These people whom I allow into my home, to spend time with my children and me, are very special. They are part of our family and make the family bigger and better.

I'm judged, too, for my willingness, in business, to partner and joint-venture with others. I don't get that. Why keep my world small? I want to expand the pie. I'm extremely selective about the people with whom I work. Similarly, they're careful about allowing me into their worlds. Eventually, once we get through the meet and greet and the enrolling process, I find amazing partners.

If you want more energy, if you want that energy to be revving optimally high, if you want to be calm and certain, then you need support. Consider presidents, queens, kings, or CEOs. You rarely see them harried and frantic, or tired and depleted. Yet they're running entire countries and corporations. The key to

great, positive energy is support and community. I\
it alone, yet too often people are surrounded by ot\
underutilized. Although it's fine to be self-reliant, it\
that leads to frustration, loneliness, and resentment. What's better
is to be resourceful. The ability to delegate, to ask for and receive
support, is a lifesaving gift.

I get a lot done because I outsource. I allow others into my life
to support me, and I'm invited into their lives to support them.
The most effective teams consist of mutually supportive members.
In my organization, teams interconnect in many Olympic-like circles, strengthening the chains of the entire community.

If You Don't Have Time, You Need a Team

Finding team, and asking for support, is vital. Unfortunately,
though, I've often heard a variation on the following:

"Loral, I've got ∞EOE∞ down."

"Okay, great. What does that mean?"

"Well, I can change the conversation; I've been turning all the
rules upside down."

"Good. And?"

"I spend a lot of time cultivating my commitment to faith. I
also feel my confidence and certainty growing. I give my dreams
my attention."

"Yay. And?"

"I'm working to uncover all my gifts. That's taking time."

"But you're finding some nice surprises, I bet."

"Indeed."

"Okay . . . and?"

"And I'm finally getting a handle on sequencing what I need
to do and when and how."

"Okay, good."

"And it's just going really well, Loral. I feel like a lot has shifted
for me, so I really don't think I need all that support and team you
talk about."

"What?! Are you serious?"

"Well, it's just, you know, I have a lot of gifts and abilities, and I just find that when I delegate, well, no one ever does it as well as I do."

"No one ever does what as well as you? Everything?"

"Well, no, but . . ."

Although people like this might be on a momentary high from discovering their Yes! Energy, it doesn't last. In fact, this path quickly leads to exhaustion and anger. The *Energy Equation* is not a short-term pick-me-up idea. This is about long-term ∞EOE∞. There's a reason for each of the eight factors in the formula. None can be skipped, and none can be ignored.

No one can do everything. No one knows everything. In fact, most people know very little, so those who do everything themselves are doomed. Community and collaboration can create monster potential. But you can't just build any community or collaborate with just anyone. A great friend might not be such a terrific teammate. Or someone who's a perfect colleague in one situation might not be suited to another. The best way to support optimal energy is to build a dream team, made up of individuals on whom you can count; with whom you can prosper; and alongside of whom you can generate positive, mutually beneficial energy.

I believe in supporting every area and part of your life—at work and home. By doing less alone, everyone can achieve more together.

There are many important facets of building and having a good support system, a great team, and a beneficial community:

— Look at what you need, and where you need it. In order to begin building the right team, you have to know what type of support you need and whom you need to do it. At times, I've seen people partner up on business ventures with their friends. In these situations, there is often one leader who is driving the project and gathering buddies and pals to help out. The seed is usually: "I have this great idea—let's do it together." Inevitably, the friends do not have complementary skill sets, and the original leader is both driving the idea and doing all the work.

I witnessed a terrible situation once when three friends got together to start a company and license a product, based on one person's idea, into an LLC. They organized the entity so that each participant represented a third. Which meant the three participants equally and legally owned the original person's intellectual property. As the project progressed, the partner with the idea wanted to sell the product to another company. The two other partners, though, felt that it was worth holding on to it. Not only did they veto the sale, but they did nothing to help develop or market the business. Nor would they let the partner with the idea have it back. Worse, the two partners suggested that the "idea" partner buy *them* out, despite the fact that they'd done absolutely nothing to that point.

More interesting, though, is that when I share this cautionary tale, the common response is: "Oh, that would never happen with my friends and me."

When money is made, all sorts of things change. I can't tell you the number of times clients have come to me to share a story similar to the one I just told. Usually we have to get my team of entity specialists, legal experts, and management professionals involved to help them untangle the problem. This involves, among other things, digging back into how the business was set up, restructuring these businesses into legal corporate entities, drawing up requisite documents and contracts, and creating a proper sequence of next business steps to move forward cleanly. It serves everyone better if all of this is done properly from the start.

I've had a lot of friends, and I've built a lot of teams. The two don't need to collide. Fortunately, because my teams become such a big part of my life, the great people on them usually *become* my friends.

When building a team, first consider *what* you need, then find *who* you need. Too many mistakes are made by getting that backward. If you try to fit a square peg in a round hole, everyone will be stuck.

I consider each objective in my life and think:

- *What type of community or team am I going to create to get that?*
- *Who, exactly, is going to help me get there?*

Like me, you probably don't need a cheerleader or someone to tell you that you can do it. Rah-rah only goes so far-far. I know I can do what I set out to do. I don't need yes-men or pep talks. I need team members who can help me get it done.

Since I know that in the future I'm always going to be building teams, I keep track of the people I meet. I have a database that includes the individuals' names, spouses' and kids' names, company names, situations in which we met, and people through whom we were introduced. I also link names to others I know. Each time I have a new need, I can reference this list.

How do you know you have the right people? You can get recommendations and so forth, but you don't really know until you're in it with them. Create experiences, use your instincts, and then cut or keep.

— **Know you know nothing.** Although you may know a lot, you don't know everything. Even if you're quick to learn, efficient at absorbing and synthesizing information, and very capable—almost freakishly so—when it comes to a wide spectrum of tasks, you can't be an expert in everything. And even if you had the potential to be all things to all people, no one has *time* to do everything, learn everything, or know everything. To build team, you must gather the skills, information, and gifts you lack.

I constantly consult other experts. Because I have certainty and confidence, I also have *enough ego to have no ego* when it comes to building team. What I do have is the belief in my own leadership. If I don't know how to do something, why would I expend valuable time and energy trying to figure it out?

Many people don't do half the things they're trying to do very well. But there are plenty of experts out there. In the same way that you don't have to know how the TV works to turn it on, how to grow vegetables to eat them, or how to make a dress to wear one, you don't have to know every single thing about business to run a successful one. Sure, it's nice for the MBAs to take classes in marketing, sales, finance, operations, and management . . . but those are just classes, and they are only learning bits and pieces. Each executive need not be an expert in each field, but only needs to find someone who is. That's you. You are your own executive— the CEO of your life, your home, your work, your ventures. The best team has capable people, so you need to surround yourself with experts.

— **Model, but don't compare.** When supercharging a life and a business, it helps to *model* others who have the type of support and community for which you're looking. Consider the people and families who seem to have a lot of energy, enjoy their time, and engage in life. Ask them what it is they do to have that calm and collected approach you admire. It's important, though, not to look side by side and compare yourself to others. Everyone has a different situation, with different needs, and different experiences. A family that might seem to have it all—including a housekeeper, a butler, and a chauffeur—may have inherited that world or bought into it for the artifice. Those teams may seem helpful, but don't actually add any calm or help create enjoyment or abundance.

Make sure the models you pick truly represent the type of team you want to have. Engage those families or businesses in conversations that help you understand their values and goals. Not every team is a good one. You want yours to be great, so *model great.*

— **Get a terrific home team.** I have the number one home team. It's not large or sophisticated, but it's wonderful. Each person who comes into my house shares my values and my goals. While an individual may not share my perspective on everything, his or her views often add to, rather than undermine, my awareness. If the people in my world are not "additive," I subtract them quickly.

Especially in my home. My kids are the most important part of my life, so my home is sacred—and the team there has to be the best of the best. I've seen others with money to throw around hire people to work in their homes after just a short interview. That makes no sense to me. I don't want hired help. I want team members and community. If it takes a village, then I want a friendly, smart, fun, engaged, energetic, happy village. Anyone who comes into my family's life must be an asset to us. Same with my business. Those with whom I work trust me to create a safe, happy, prosperous community.

There are too many people who make things much more difficult than they need to be. They want to live a life that's expansive and fun, but they put so much judgment on themselves that they're not willing to get support at home.

Change the conversation. If you want more energy and a shift in your attitude, stop wasting your talents. If you want more time with your kids, spouse, and friends, then relinquish the tasks that take up that time, and let others support and help you.

— Don't clean your own house. Along the same lines, anyone who wastes their time and energy doing what they can outsource doesn't value their own time and energy. It's not that I don't value housecleaning—in fact, I value it greatly. That's why I outsource it to someone who can do it better than I can. Not only am I supporting another business or individual, but in the time it takes me to clean my house the way I want it cleaned, I could be taking my kids skiing or getting a deal completed for wealth building. Both of those activities reward me much more than I pay out.

When I work with people who tell me they want to generate wealth, one of the first questions I ask them, after inquiries about their current financial literacy, is if they clean their own homes. If they say yes, I know they're not ready to get serious about generating wealth or expanding their lives. Those dozens of hours every week devoted to cleaning, landscaping the yard, or doing chores around the house could be spent selling a product or service, polishing up ideas for a new product, or marketing a new opportunity. When you enroll others, you're buying back your time to make more cash, build your business, and expand your life.

Although cleaning your own home may seem like such a little thing, the time spent on even the smallest things, such as this, add up to big depletions of your energy and can weigh heavily on your attitude.

— Do what you're good at, and stop doing what you hate to do and aren't good at anyway. The best, highest use of your time is doing what you do well. If you're good at many things, whittle down the list so you can focus on the tasks that feed your energy and attitude.

If you think you're not good at much, that's probably not true. Take a minute to think about certain tasks you do that come easily and that usually have a good outcome. Many people overlook their skills and talents only because they're so obvious.

More important, consider the things you do every day that are draining your energy and attitude. It's vital to your ∞EOE∞ not to do these things anymore. If they feel like life "have-to's," carefully consider the reality of that. Then consider if you can build a team, or partner with someone else, to help you do those things. Often there are others who don't like, or aren't good at, things at which you excel, and vice versa. Exchanging skill sets is a great way to start building team.

When I did personal training in college, I had so many jobs that I was working 16 hours a week, in addition to playing sports and taking on a full course load. I liked being a personal trainer, and I was good at it. I was also good at sharing the message about my services, and as a result, I had more people wanting my services than I had time to provide them.

Of course, because of my mantra, I said yes to each and every client, assuming I'd figure out how to deal with each of them later. Soon, though, I realized that the highest, best use of my time was in marketing the company. I decided to build a team and hire other people to do the personal training, while I created and ran the company. Next thing I knew, I'd replaced myself on the frontlines of the business and had a nice-size company generating some respectable revenue.

The bonus—I was working less and making more money. Not only that, but my classmates who were good at teaching aerobics and personal training but had no idea how to market themselves were thrilled to get the jobs from me. The venture got bigger and bigger, with me doing less and less. You can bet the money fueled my energy and optimism. Teams were working out pretty great for me.

— Be in control, without being controlling. My team knows they can do things better than I can, and I let them . . . that's the biggest gift I give my team. I manage, but I don't micromanage. I lead, but I don't hover. I control, but I'm not controlling.

Certain and calm energy inspires and drives a team. Leaders who have to touch every little detail are insecure. Those who try to fix every single car of the train themselves to get it back on track usually find that it never gets moving again. It's a big mistake to think that no one else can do things as well as you can. What if they can't? Maybe you're right, you're a big superhero person who does everything better than everyone else. But how, in a 24-hour day, are you going to do it all? If you want abundance and fulfillment, if you want ∞EOE∞, you have to get out of the way of your own ego. Those who don't delegate, who end up doing everything themselves, eventually end up angry, frustrated, and resentful.

When considering the teams for various areas of your life, think about what part of the *doing* can be yours and what part you can delegate. If you trust yourself, you can trust others to be smarter and more capable in certain arenas. *It's not easy being a superhero, so why do it?*

If you have "Superior Attitude Syndrome," then team building is not going to work for you. Consider that for a moment. Do you recognize this trait in yourself? If so, then take a minute to forgive yourself, pat yourself on the back, and put yourself in a new conversation.

- **Fact:** No one will do the work like you do.
  That's fine. But they're going to do it their way, and they're going to get it done.

- **Fact:** You want things done your way.
  That's fine. But wouldn't you rather be in action, with the help of others, than alone in your own controlled "perfection paralysis"?

- **Fact:** You've never built a team before, so you don't really know who's available to help you out there.
  That's fine. Take the time to look around and get some help. There may be people who do things better than you.

But whatever you do . . .

— Do not partner sideways or down; partner up. If you're going to take the time to build a team, build the right one. If you don't know how to do something, don't hire someone else who doesn't know how to do it either. You want a skilled team.

Equally important, if you find someone who has the skills you need, do not hire that person unless he or she fits the culture of your team. While differing perspectives and various views help enrich a team, you want the basic core values of each member of the team to be in line. If one bad apple doesn't have integrity or value honesty, the entire bunch can rot.

You also want to get mentors and models on the team who've been where you want to go. You do not want to be the biggest fish in the pond. If you want your business to be a $5 million business, you need systems in place to support that level of revenue. If you've never done it before, you need a team member who has— someone who can lead that type of investment, development, and marketing.

Although I partner up when I bring in different people to my various teams, it's important that none of the members feel more-than or less-than. We keep it very horizontal. We also have a "No jerks" policy. Several years ago, I made a rule: I only hang out with cool people. That may sound very seventh grade, but by "cool people," I mean good, solid folks. There's no room for whiny people. When I see that, I have to remove my energy from that gross space.

Can you imagine a community that's made up of only the people you admire and respect? That's what I did. I imagined it, and it happened.

If someone brings in an attitude or an air that's not in line with that of the prevailing culture, we ask that individual to leave immediately. Quickly *transitioning* good team members in and bad team members out is vital to keeping the community healthy. My teams are made up of the greatest groups of people. We have this *connectivity* and *congruency* that creates a brilliant dance among all the members. Although we have different opinions, we're all having the same kind of conversation. We trust each other to argue well. We create debates and fight together to get to the best idea in the room.

— **Make team building continuous.** There have been times when I've been complacent about my teams. I built such a great group that I took my eye off the ball. This happened with a marketing and sales company to which I was outsourcing some of our work. Initially, the team was great. Then as we grew, I had less of my internal folks involved with those partners. Before I knew it, the company had made promises to customers that did not fit with our values. They were diminishing and changing the brand, using its name for products I didn't approve. We were locked into a contract. I spent a lot of time untangling a mess that, if I'd watched a smidgen more carefully, wouldn't have gotten all knotted up in the first place.

Once, I had someone on my team who I knew would help our community, but at that point he just wasn't. He wasn't leading, he wasn't motivating, he wasn't accountable, he wasn't supportive. This didn't seem in line with his character, so I was mystified by it. Then I realized that he was in the wrong position. He had, as Jim

Collins explains in his book *Good to Great: Why Some Companies Make the Leap . . . and Others Don't,* the wrong seat on the bus.

This team member had many gifts, but we weren't exploiting them properly. He was creative and technical, and I moved him to a position in our marketing department. His reaction: "I don't know anything about marketing."

Now? He's leading that department. Although I believe in transitioning quickly, when you hire a good person who doesn't seem to be working out, don't fire him or her too fast. That individual may be serving the wrong function in the organization.

Additionally, whether on the business team or the home team, don't put too many activities that are unrelated on one person. If you give database duties to someone in accounting, don't also give him sales-related tasks. If you jam too many unrelated tasks on one person, he will fail.

— **Play on strengths and protect energy.** During the time I was threatened by lawsuits and suffered attacks on my brand, it didn't help my energy and optimism to obsess on these things. Fortunately, my team helped here as well. They shielded me against negative and draining forces, activities, and people. I engaged experienced lawyers who realized I was being taken for a ride, they took over the day-to-day on the lawsuits, and I stood back. I hired Internet experts who knew how to navigate the search engines and websites and let them deal with the brand. If I spent any part of my day on the negative energy coming my way, I'd deplete my own energy. As a priority, I always protect my energy.

Dealing with aggression and attacks is not one of my strengths. I don't have a talent for confronting dark energy. Instead of scolding myself for being sensitive—a gift I use to my advantage—I find others to take on the tasks that aren't my strengths. It's important that I not let myself get entwined in the messiness of the ugly behaviors of others. As long as I remain candid, and in integrity, I can support my positive energy. My energy is never at risk, because I won't let it be. Some members of my team act as a fortress against bad vibes and meanness. They don't even share their day-to-day reports; they just get the job done. Many more members of the team focus on the positive. We nurture and cultivate the good things we want our community to be.

This is true for the entire team. We create a supportive network where strengths are emphasized and weaknesses are handed off to others. This not only allows people to be the best team members they can, but it makes them 100 percent accountable and supportive if they're working in their best light. I constantly line up people's brains around the community, getting the best minds I can to go do what they do.

— **Lead like you've never led before.** If you're going to have extreme optimism and energy, you need a team; and if you want a team, you need to be a great leader. This means caring about your community and the people with whom you work enough to make sure your teams look out for the best interests of everyone involved. No one on the team should be doing you any favors by being there. Nor you them. All should feel that the team and the community you're building is the best for them. The people who work in sales for me want to do sales. The people who schedule my appointments find fulfillment in that task. These tasks work for them, so that does, indeed, work for all of us.

My business is a train that won't stop. We keep building momentum and critical mass because a lot of folks are hopping on board, driving the engine. I've seen other organizations die because they don't care about their people or the community they're building. We don't allow arrogance on any of my teams. We don't allow small, divisive thinking. We don't keep secrets or have separate dialogues. Transparency and communication are key. Because we are all about expanding the pie to make a bigger opportunity for each and every person involved, we continue to attract the best of the best.

And we get even better if we do the right thing at the right time. . . .

∞EOE∞

CHAPTER 13

The Inquiry:

What kind of teams and support can you use in your life?

The Exercise:

1. Think about various areas of your life. In which parts could you replace yourself with others who could do the same task more efficiently?

2. Consider your home. How are you supported in that arena? Who does most of the work there, and how can all the members of the household have their lives better supported?

3. Think about all the must-do tasks in your day, week, month. Which activities are energy enriching? Which are depleting? What puts you in a better mood? What create negativity? How can you get support in the areas that do not help your energy or attitude?

Next Steps

Consider individuals, families, and businesses that seem to have it all. Connect with up to three of these people over the next week and ask them about the support and teams in their lives.

Talk to your family about how you can operate better as a team. See if there are others you can bring into your village to make it a happier, more fulfilling place.

Look at your business or your job. Think about how you can be better supported, or be better at supporting others, to make the pie big enough for everyone.

THE SEQUENCING CATALYST

The Right Thing at the Right Time

The final factor of the *Energy Equation* is *sequencing*—the essence of *leadership*. This one tactic can turn an average leader into a great one. It can also help *you* do well in leading your own life. Sequencing is the idea that *the right steps at the right time get you where you want to go.* It is an essential catalyst for energy and attitude.

I play every situation in my head before I get into it. That's typical of athletes, and I'm sure I'm one of many who've carried that over into my business world. I also sequence in the everyday of my life, not just for meetings or other business situations.

I begin each day with visualization—planning the day, and then the months and years, ahead of me. This affects not just my business community, but my family and friends. Sequencing, doing the right thing, at the right time, can contribute to every area of life. By taking the time to *think* ahead of a situation, you *get* ahead of it, and then every situation flows easier and more efficiently.

Often, people understand where they are and know where they want to go, but the sequence of steps from here to there eludes them. They proceed forward, only to: (a) make too many wrong turns, (b) circle around one step, or (c) spend too long in that inefficient 20 percent (remember the 80-20 rule).

Proper sequencing is probably one of the most important steps in life and in business. People who know how to efficiently get from here to there, who can see their way through a process, are more effective than most.

In his seminal and widely popular 1984 book *The Goal: A Process of Ongoing Improvement,* Eliyahu Goldratt examined operating efficiencies in systems management. His findings, shared through a fictional tale, are applicable both in and outside of business. The basic idea, his Theory of Constraints, was that by clearly seeing through a process, we can manage constraints and utilize capacity to eliminate bottlenecks and create a better flow. Goldratt even uses the analogy of a Boy Scout troop to explain how the placement of kids, the order, can affect the productivity of the entire group. The proper sequencing of people and activities keeps systems moving properly.

A key part of Goldratt's observation is the idea of "dependent events," which means the end result of one step affects the next, or that the output of the first activity affects the input into the second. Each link in a sequence depends on the one that came before it and affects the one that comes after it. This is apparent in any sequence of events. As you go through your day, if the line at the coffee shop is too long, you'll be late for your first meeting; if that meeting runs late, the noon deadline of a project analysis is shot . . . and on and on.

Dependent events can also be emotional. If your morning starts off rotten, this fluctuation, if uncontrolled, can ripple through your whole day, keeping you moody from start to finish. Because such flows have momentum, the overall effect of one problem becomes much greater than the initial event that triggered it—almost like the theoretical "butterfly effect" in chaos theory (which, oversimplified, states that a small disruption in one place can wreak havoc elsewhere). Proper and efficient sequencing can keep chaos out of one's day or a business.

Three Days to Fast Cash

I've used the idea of sequencing for most of my life. As I mentioned before, I have this telepathic sense of how to get people onto their fastest path to cash, because I can see, very clearly, the steps they need to take to make money immediately. In fact, I have a seminar called 3 Days To Cash where people learn to create fast cash, daily. By the end of that weekend, every single person in the room has found a way to shift their business idea into a realistic, money-generating Cash Machine. This is done by creating a sequence of:

1. Defining one's skill set.
2. Modeling a similar business idea.
3. Creating a sellable revenue model.
4. Devising a fast marketing plan.
5. Enlisting a team.
6. Asking for cash to seal the deal.

Although this may be an unusual talent, getting people into cash generation fast, the idea that I can sequence steps is not. There are many people who are inherently good at seeing the path from idea to goal. They are often producers or plant managers or mothers. What I've found interesting, though, is that many times those with this talent don't apply it to other areas of their lives. They can put together a concert with the proper load-in, setup, and load-out of equipment, but at home, the cardboard boxes are still unpacked, the laundry's piling up, and the important talk that needed to happen before the in-laws arrived was overlooked.

The Sequencing Support Systems

There are many ways to employ sequencing to support your energy and attitude. . . .

Communication

Proper sequencing can save a marriage. Or any relationship. When a conversation begins with affirmations, leading into the difficult issues, the information is more easily received.

Good teachers know how to communicate in a proper sequence. If they give their students too much to do at once, the learning becomes overwhelming. If they teach too little, the students become bored. If they have a poor order of lesson plans, the students are confused. A proper, well-built-upon syllabus—a sequence of learning—allows for an efficient and effective flow of information, resulting in a better education.

A good spouse or partner in a relationship tries to sequence his or her communication. If six chores need to get done, it might be best to present the idea of planning to go to a movie after the "honey do" list is complete. If a camping trip with pals is desired, it might be best to first suggest scheduling a future trip for two to a spa.

Sequencing of communication is not manipulative or passive-aggressive. It's done in a straightforward manner, with a thoughtful consideration of the listener's ability to absorb the information. Thinking of how the information will be received before it's given ensures that a proper sequence of communication, in any situation, can be delivered.

Action

Proper sequencing can be all the difference between failure and success in any endeavor. For instance, in many start-up companies, you have to *sell first*. This is a step too many companies miss or skip, and then they have problems right away. Having 300 units of a perfectly prepared product sitting in your garage depletes both optimism and energy. Having 300 orders for almost-completed, not-yet-perfected products spurs action. As I said, it still amazes me to see people get it right at their jobs, where they've been trained to follow a certain protocol, and then leave that skill set at work instead of applying that ability to *sequence* to other areas of their lives.

Planning

The reason why so many ventures fail before they get off the ground is because they get stuck in the planning process. Mapping out one's entire sequence means that nothing will happen. Action—and by this I mean *sales*—must occur as part of, not following, the planning sequence.

While architects draft plans for a new building, construction is under way to demolish the old structure and dig the new foundation. If everyone waited for each person to complete and fully polish his or her step, the bottlenecks would forestall the success of the process. The architect might draft an initial idea, but if every member of the crew waited until the last doilies were drawn on the rooftops, the ground floor would never get constructed, and the project would burn through cash before the first rock was moved.

Similarly, in video-game design, the scripts are written but not perfected before development begins. In the entertainment industry, writers keep polishing the ideas even while the costume and set designers are drawing up their execution.

In my community, plans aren't even the first step in a sequence. We begin with the goal so as to create incentive and motivate. Then we jump into immediate action to create results based on what it is we think we want to do.

Too many entrepreneurs spend the first part of their sequence on business plans, and never get the venture off the ground. It's important to start with sales to see if someone wants to buy the product or service. Then, when you do all that work, at least you know you're creating something for which there is a market.

That Dumb Debt Conversation

Doing the wrong things at the wrong time is a major energy—and attitude and cash—depleter. ∞EOE∞ relies heavily on sequencing. Doing the right thing at the right time not only *saves* time, energy, and emotional turmoil, but it greases wheels of action so that you get into results faster.

One sequence that too many are getting wrong right now is that they are cutting and saving instead of generating and creating new cash to get above the fear. The wrong first step is getting out of debt. People need to realize that getting out of debt gets you to . . . well, nothing. You'll feel better having accomplished the goal, but you'll sure miss your lattes. Worse, there's a good chance you'll get back in the red again.

I'm not saying not to worry about debt, because you do need to manage it or it will sabotage your energy and gifts. But the best way to get out of a hole and into financial health is to learn to sell and generate more cash. If you focus on your debt first, you'll just be sitting on the floor in an empty living room munching on celery. If you focus on your skills and gifts to create value and a new enterprise, your debt will be eliminated *and* you'll have a new, exciting, energizing venture. More important, once you get a handle on this sequence, you will never go into the debt cycle again. A new sequence will change your entire relationship with money.

The sequence of debt relief goes like this: get small, give up the good things in life, scrimp, save, and be sad. The proper sequence for eliminating debt has a different set of steps. Instead of giving up what you want in order to *get* what you want, you'll think: *What am I going to create to get what I need, and who is going to help me get there?*

It's a sequence of changing the conversation, relying on faith and certainty, having the confidence to stay in your dreams, uncovering gifts to create value, and using a team to get going and get results.

The Right Sequence for the Right Situation

The proper sequencing is unique to each activity and person. Each person needs an individualized sequence to meet his or her goals. For many businesses, sales is the first step, followed by team building.

Now, as I said, I've been criticized for emphasizing team early in the entrepreneurial process.

It's not unusual to hear something like: "Really, Loral, I'm supposed to hire 30 people when I don't have a penny to my name?"

This reaction is a clear misunderstanding of the concept of team and totally dismisses the idea of sequencing. If just one person helps you with a task you don't do well, and in turn you help him or her with something that comes easily to you, you've begun to capture the essence of team. It's a buildup into a new conversation. I'm not suggesting that you become the general manager of your own professional, highly paid squad. That's the wrong conversation and the wrong sequence.

The benefits, versus the costs, of generating sales and then creating a team as a first-then-second step are many. Most of the wealthy know this—*they* do not go it alone. They can't. No one can. While your first step is to generate cash-in, the second step is, as I've said, to use that cash-in to get help, immediately. Whether that help is in the home or in the business doesn't matter, as long as it frees up your time to generate more sales and more cash. The mistake too many people make is that as soon as they make some cash, they pay off debt or buy equipment. That's the wrong sequence. First cash-in should go to buy more time to generate more cash. Team creates that time.

In some situations, your first step may be to change the conversation. If for too long you've thought that you were stuck in your life and trapped in an existence that saps your energy and threatens your attitude, then you need to flip that conversation to empowerment. The second step may be recognizing your gifts and seeing how you can better plug into your ability to do more for yourself and create your own value.

Sequencing is an efficient, essential catalyst. The *Energy Equation* formula itself can work in any sequence for any situations, but it's vital that you choose the *right* sequence for the *right* situation.

The Sequence at Home

Let's consider the home. There are so many parents who would love to know that a life of calm and ease in the home is attainable. Many of us make life so hard. It *is* hard—if you let it be. How can families, couples . . . even busy singles . . . pull out of the chaos, get supported, and live lives that are fulfilling and happy?

The priority at home should be 100 percent love, of course, but the approach should not be 100 percent emotional. If we allow life to come at us, on its terms, it will be chaotic. But if we prepare for situations, with visualization and sequencing of clear and logical steps, we can be ahead of those situations, and live them more slowly.

That's what athletes do when they visualize. For most beginning athletes, the world of their sport starts out very fast. It's only when the game begins to slow down that they can master it. Now, obviously, the speed of the game has not really changed. It's just their perception of it. That's the art of being a good athlete—slowing the game down. That's the science of sequencing—slowing life down.

At home, this begins right away. You have a choice when you wake up. Are your mornings jarring? Do they start with resistance? Do you bang pots and pans, scramble to cook breakfast, make a quick pot of coffee, or scream for the kids to get a move on? Or is it more gentle and framing? Do you have time to relax—snuggle with your spouse, perhaps—and discuss the day ahead? I imagine you may have laughed out loud at the latter suggestion. But it's possible to change the conversation, get into the calm sequencing of Yes! Energy, and change your days.

Consider creating a day that goes like this: Set your alarm for 30 minutes before you need to get up. Before you go exercise, tend to your family, or start getting ready for work, think about how you want the day to go. Consider that you are choosing to be the best you can be that day—to be happy, to be joyful, to be positive.

Now, you might be reading this and already feel the resentment that comes with defending one's position.

"What are you talking about, Loral? I've been doing it all, and I *have* to do it all or it won't get done."

I understand that most of us can't admit or believe that we've been doing something wrong our whole lives. We haven't. But the way in which most of us have been operating—the busy, but not productive, overscheduled lives—isn't working.

Chances are, you've never had the time, or the energy, to step back from the "way it's always been" . . . the way your parents or your bosses have run their lives. But the old way and the new world have collided.

It's high time to take charge, lead our lives, and commit to finding a better way. That's the entire point of the sequencing catalyst. It's new, it's evolved, and it provides that better way.

The Tactics of Sequencing

So, how does one sequence?

The end product is that you think or write out the actual process in which you will, in the future, engage. There are several ways to approach this exercise. You can start at the beginning of a situation, the middle, the end, or some mix of those. The gist is that you mentally step into a scenario before you actually live it out so that you can consider, see, and then set up the steps for success.

You can sequence any type of situation, from an important but dreaded conversation with a friend or colleague to a six-month preproduction schedule for a new project.

I recommend a combination of three steps to sequencing:

1. View it.

2. Undo it.

3. Time it out.

View It: Visualize

The idea here, as I've mentioned, is that you put yourself into the situation and play it out before it happens, the way athletes do. By the time a swimmer is up on the blocks, he has already seen himself dive off the block, swim underwater, pull through his strokes, flip the turn, return, and touch the wall, swimming the entire race to the finish in his mind before it's even started. A sprinter will stand on the side of the track and see herself running around each corner, taking the inside lane. I used to play the whole first quarter of my basketball games in the locker room, making plays in my head, getting shots off before the buzzer.

This can work well in everyday life as well. The issue for most people, though, is that it takes time. They feel silly previewing an event. Or they think it's a waste of precious time when they need to just get to it. But if you get into it, you will see that the time spent up front does so much more than save you time in the long run. It empowers you energetically. Visualization can make any conversation, activity, event, or situation flow much more smoothly. Just as the proper sequencing of operations on a factory floor can increase efficiencies, visualizing the right steps in the right order can optimize the outcome of any event. Similarly, for a conversation, visualizing the right topics at the right time, as well as the desired, if generally open-ended, outcome can increase the effectiveness of your agenda.

Undo It: Reverse Technology

When a company tries to understand the product of its competitors, it employs reverse technology, where it literally takes apart a product to understand how it's put together. Chefs and even amateur foodies, of course, do this, too, uncovering recipes and ingredients by dissecting the entrée.

In sequencing, you can do this visually. By considering the end product, the end result you desire, you can break it apart—"dissect the recipe"—to see what steps would need to occur to create that outcome. The unraveling then becomes the sequence of steps for putting it back together.

Time It Out: Future Pacing

Once you know what you want to do and the steps you need to take, it helps then to time them out or schedule them backward. Even with a simple conversation with someone, I consider how much time I have to talk, what I want the outcome to be, and how much time I have, going in reverse, to hit each point on the agenda. With projects, I look ahead several months, years sometimes, and then walk back along a timeline to make sure I can hit each target in time to do the next step. This provides a bird's-eye view from which to lead the project.

A Flexible Approach

Flexibility and adaptability are vital to sequencing. If you set each step in stone, you lose the opportunity to go with the flow. Sequencing is a framework, not a cage. If it becomes too rigid, if you're a slave to your sequence, then you will actually deplete your energy.

As I mentioned earlier, I keep my purpose ahead of my output, which means that I go into a situation with an idea of what I want to accomplish, and then I create a sequence to get there. But since I'm not alone in the conversation, and I like to engage at Level III listening, I need to remain open to the inputs around the room. If I've developed a sequence that has a good amount of give, this usually works out just fine. Some people who are very adept at sequencing can build many paths, simultaneous sequences, so that they can hop from one to the other as necessary.

Sequencing is a specific skill set that needs to be put into action and experienced in order to be understood. Once you get the hang of it, though, your energy and attitude will reach all-new levels, and you'll be ready to master the *Energy Equation*.

Similarly, once you get the hang of the *Energy Equation,* you'll be able to do less, make more. . . .

∞EOE∞

CHAPTER 14

The Inquiry:

Consider a situation or conversation in which you need to accomplish something. What is the outcome you want to achieve?

The Exercise:

1. Define and write out where you are at the beginning of the imagined scenario.

2. Define and write out where you want to be at the end. What's your goal or objective?

3. Write out the best sequence of steps you think you should take to get from beginning to end. Start out by visualizing the actual event occurring. Then work in reverse, from the end to the beginning. Finally, pace out the steps you need to take and the time in which you can take them.

Next Steps:

Get into action with respect to sequencing. Consider a short-term situation or conversation or event you need to plan. Set up a sequence of possible steps. View it. Undo it. Time it out. And then try it.

DO LESS, MAKE MORE

Freedom Days

I've watched people in the best of circumstances get depressed, and I've seen those who've lost everything participate in life with unmitigated joy. I'm sure genetics and chemistry and conditioning are responsible, but then that leaves us, again, with only one question: *So what—now what?*

The goal of Yes! Energy is to generate and sustain the constant flow of positive solution orientation. The objective is to capture that ∞EOE∞ and then find a way to maintain it for the rest of your life.

The strategy?

Harness the power of the core vibration and spiral up into a virtuous cycle.

As I mentioned, my community and I move fast. We have so much we want to do and be that we just can't help ourselves. A lot of it is because I refuse to compromise my vision. I know how great we can all be, so I push the train to move at 200 miles an hour. Whenever I'm told by a fearful few to slow down, I say "No way." It's my train, so it's my speed. If others don't like it or feel threatened by it, they don't need to judge me; they can get off the train and get out of its way. But most stay on. The energy and excitement are infectious. Once people get "infected" by my pace, my efficiency, and my contagious energy, there is no slowing them down either.

We get things done. I say "do," they go. They say "do," *I* go. It's a mutual, noncompromising, like-minded, fabulous state of mind. I love it.

What's great, too, is that as we build, grow, and move forward, we're actually doing less and making more. We get so efficient and the momentum grows so powerful that the outputs far exceed our inputs. It's a whirl of productivity and engagement. As I said, I love it.

Imagine it for a moment. Imagine being in the midst of positive, infectious, optimistic energy—all the time. Because we create a business, an organization, and a global community where congruency is key, there's little tension or dissension. We are consistent in what we do. We line up; we're connected; and we stay in the circle of our capacity, our character, and our vision.

Do things go wrong? Every day. Are there fights? Every week. Do some people cry? Well, no, not really. But the mistakes and the conflicts are part of the process. Because we move fast, we also quickly weed out those who diminish our Yes! Energy. If people are having the wrong conversation, or not coming from a faith-based place of confidence and certainty—stomping on others' dreams; diminishing their own or others' gifts; and not participating as valuable, respectful, supportive, and positive members of the team—they are asked to improve fast or leave.

We have a high tolerance for mistakes or wrong turns, and are equally understanding when someone is in the wrong spot to utilize his or her strengths, but is willing to move. What is key, though, is that each person understand the *Energy Equation* and learn how to use, be in, and help *others* be in extreme optimism and energy.

Turning Energy into Abundance

My vision is that everyone in our society gets to a place where they click into leading their own lives. Where they feel motivated and inspired and kick their own butts for compromising.

For some—dare I say dumb—reason, many of us are taught that our pursuits must be a zero-sum game, that some must win and some must lose. I flat-out do not believe that.

I built an organization that works to create the win-win for everyone. What I've found is that in our wealth-building communities, the little microeconomies we've created through our mutually beneficial businesses, everyone is offering and everyone is receiving. It works all around, just as it did in the small-economy societies of old, when farmers, merchants, butchers, bakers, and candlestick makers sold goods and services to each other. Few had jobs, or trudged off to work for "the Man." Most had their own ventures and led their own lives. The majority of those who did the work of others were slaves, serfs, and indentured servants. *There* is a comparison.

Unfortunately, because so many have bought into the industrial-age model of "get a job," the disparity of wealth on this planet has become astonishing. This is unnecessary. There's no reason why the world can't become an abundant marketplace in which everyone buys from and sells to each other. The reason that doesn't work now is because there are too many people with jobs who are happy to use any extra cash to buy a 42-inch HD TV and eat fast food. They are not motivated to create, develop, or build, as were those who came before us. Imagine if that level of luxury and satisfaction was available to the early American colonists. We'd have no new industry, no innovative products, and the West would end halfway across Pennsylvania.

In my vision, the world becomes a marketplace where everyone can create, and then buy from and sell to each other. They also invest in and support each other to develop and grow.

I've heard people say that this approach takes a lot of time. It does, at first. But once you learn how to get support and create team, you find you have more time. Eventually, you will *do less, make more.* When you establish a team, you create a whole new world for yourself. Instead of having friends who want to sit around playing video games, go shopping, or hang out and read magazines, you'll have friends who want to join forces to invent, innovate, create, debate, develop, and explore. Now that's fun. That's energizing. That's the community in which I live.

Too many people go about entrepreneurship in all the wrong ways. They start or buy a small business and think they're on their way. But all they've done is bought themselves another job. Only worse. They get so exhausted and overwhelmed that they can't even find time to stay organized. Now, instead of going to a job, they *live* in the job, papers and files piling up around the house. Yuck. All this just to bring in $60,000 to $100,000 a year.

You've got to get past that way of thinking. The choices are not: (a) have a job, (b) buy a small business, or (c) become an entrepreneur and go it alone. The goal is not $100,000. The new conversation is to get into a team or create a community where you can build a vision together. Where you can make *several hundred* thousand dollars. Where you can generate and maintain wealth. If you sit in this little space of old choices, you will get stuck and stay small.

The people I know who've made a lot of money and changed their lives are both highly motivated and dislike the norm. They took risks that weren't even that risky to get out of the 9-to-5 corporate structure and move into leading their own lives. Consider the huge companies that exist out there that are now part and parcel of the corporate world. Those companies didn't exist before the original visionary created them. That could be you. You and your team could discover and create the new world.

Let's consider how you can get started.

ΔC—Changing the Conversation

In the old conversation, the economy relies heavily on consumption. People go to work; make money; pay a lot of that money back to the government in taxes; use most of the remaining money for food, clothes, shelter, utilities, and transportation; and then might have a small amount left over to buy discretionary items like decor for the house, more clothes, toys, or entertainment.

This is not what those in the new conversation do. Those in the new conversation model the ways of the wealthy. Not the flash-in-the-pan, conspicuous-consumption nouveau riche, but the wealthy who know that a dollar is best used to create another dollar. The wealthy have enough money to buy whatever they want. Yet they don't just go and buy 800 ice-cream sundaes. Consumption gets boring after a while. That's why some have art all over the walls—they like to invest in long-term, accumulating wealth.

For those who want to be a part of this new conversation, the *sequence* of steps to model wealth building goes like this:

1. Make more money (see the "Three Days to Fast Cash" sequence in the previous chapter).

2. Set up the proper systems to support that revenue generation.

3. Retain more of the revenue through a proper entity structure.

4. Use that additional income to invest in other businesses and assets.

5. Take the passive income and invest back in your skill set and more assets.

6. Simultaneously gather and build a team so that you can replace yourself.

That's a wealth cycle, and that's how you generate wealth.

One of the first things to do in the sequence of the new conversation is to get that first step right. That's the whole focus of my 3 Days To Cash seminar. Once people get a handle on that, it's fascinating what happens. They become moneymaking machines. Their energy builds, their excitement soars, and they're on their way.

The economics of the new conversation is macroeconomics played through mini-economies. Instead of hoarding cash and resources, money and value move around. There's less consumption and more growing through investments in each other. Again, think of the cliques of the wealthy and how they got started and built big. Few did it alone; they worked together to invest in businesses, not lifestyles. In these new teams and communities, little of the goods and services are perishable trends or fickle fashions. Instead, there's value all around.

This is not unique to my teams, my organization, or my community. This type of new conversation is being had all over the world. The brave and the wealthy are constantly creating their own communities of wealth and exchange. All I'm doing, by suggesting this new conversation, is making this *old* idea of economics and community accessible to everyone.

[F(2C)*D]—Faith, Certainty, Confidence, and Dreams

It takes me all of ten seconds to recognize if someone is anchored in a bad place or centered in faith. My view is, if you're sitting on a pile of negative—if you're not happy—then the first question you need to ask yourself is: "How do I get out of this bad space I'm in?" The motivated and uncompromised ask, "What are the possibilities in the times of the impossible?"

During the past few years (from 2007 to 2010), so many lost so much that there seemed to be an abundance of nothing but surrender. The motivated and uncompromised didn't surrender, though. They reevaluated. While most looked for safety, security, and comfort, those who were certain and knew they could have something better hung on to their dreams. The motivated and uncompromised stood up to their failures and got back up after being knocked down. While the fearful and uncertain picketed and protested their company closings, waited and watched while others decided their fate, and then went back to small thinking and focused on getting yet another job, the confident dreamers continued on a path of serial entrepreneurship.

Wouldn't it be interesting if, one day, a group of laborers at a plant got together after its closing, brainstormed about a new product idea that repurposed their collective skill sets, and then partnered with a local bank—which would be equally motivated to keep the laborers prospering—to buy the plant themselves? Instead of losing, they'd be winning like they'd never won in their lives. The closing would be a beginning, not an end. They'd lead their own lives and create their own company in which they all shared ownership. All it would take would be the certainty and confidence that comes from the core of knowing cultivated from their faith.

"Oh, Loral, that's plain crazy thinking," someone might say.

Really? Why? Why is it so unbelievable to imagine that skilled workers can stop thinking of themselves as employees and shift the conversation to be owners—to lead their own lives, and commit to their own venture; to have the confidence and certainty to realize their gifts, come together as a team, and take the proper steps to pursue a better vision, a dream? Those who don't have enough faith to push out of the small into the big, to take action, don't understand the power of Yes! Energy.

G—Recognizing and Realizing Gifts

I had a lawyer come into one of my 3 Days To Cash workshops. He wanted to shift his life into ∞EOE∞. He wanted to lead; he was ready to commit; he wanted to generate more money, build a team, and do something outside of his practice. But he was stuck.

Every idea he had kept getting him back to where he'd been. He had no idea what his gifts were.

He thought about writing a book about tax law and selling it to others in the room. Fortunately, he was constrained by the mandate to generate real cash in his pocket in the next 72 hours. He wrote up a quick little report that shared his thoughts on how to better manage one's taxes. He didn't have time to tell every little secret, but he gave the basics. Not only did he find a target audience interested in paying him $20 for the report, but many people wanted a follow-up consult. He changed his revenue model to give away the brochure, with the presell of his higher-end services.

Although he had no intention of being a lawyer for much longer, he realized that he had a real skill set that he could leverage outside of his job. He could then use that skill to build a business. Once he'd learned how to build a business and run it, he could move on to build a different venture using other skill sets more in line with his new vision for himself.

Part of discovering and uncovering your gifts is to act differently in the new conversation than you did in the old. It requires becoming visible, contributing, getting out of the house, and being of service to the community and in the economy. Once you recognize your gifts and your ability to generate cash, you can stop wasting your time and energy *consuming* and get into *creating*. If you want to thrive in this new economy, you have to contribute. No one will do it for you, and there's no one better than you to do it.

T—Gathering Team and Support

There's just nothing like team. If you have one and are part of a supportive, thriving, positive community, you can do anything. Team pushes energy; team supports attitude. When I first started Live Out Loud, we focused on a program called Team Made Millionaires. We busted the myth of self-made millionaires to prove how working with others accelerated wealth. The wealthy have always known that, working together to create small communities and economies. Now it's time, in the new conversation, for anyone, anywhere, to access that same leverage.

I've been told by Wall Street investors that what I'm suggesting is too simplistic. That's exactly what makes it work. It's clear: Supply and demand, creation and investment. The same attributes of the deal making and transactions in which Wall Street engages.

In order to have ∞EOE∞, it's vital to do less, make more, which means . . . delegating. In fact, the less you do, the more you make. This is possible because it's not you wasting your time doing each and every little thing. Even a task that seems easy and quick is never easy *or* quick. Everything takes time. To be in extreme energy, you need to value your time and preserve your energy for the tasks that will help you generate wealth, expand your life, and have fun.

Every year, it seems I do less and less of what I used to do, and more and more of what's new and exciting to me. As I grow, my responsibilities shift into new frontiers, and then my businesses and my life expand even more. It's a virtuous upward cycle, all supported by team.

S—Sequencing the Right Thing at the Right Time

If I handed you $10,000 today, chances are that if you don't have an understanding of how to generate and build wealth, you would spend that money and have nothing. Or you'd save it, and that's just delayed spending. Either way, it wouldn't make you any wealthier. But if you put that money into the proper sequence described above in the wealth cycle, your money would make money, and you'd feel energized and optimistic.

Sequencing can help you all over the place in your life. This is a vital ingredient of extreme energy. A properly sequenced schedule of events can get you into ∞EOE∞ every day. If your day isn't working for you, change it. I've known salespeople who got up early and stayed up late to do their calls, even though that might not be the best time for their particular market. Yet they keep doing it their way, working hard for less. That makes no sense to me. Every community has a best time to sell. Uncover it. Learn from those who've succeeded in that market.

If you are lacking energy, if you are feeling negative, if you're not having the success you want in your life, consider shifting your patterns. Take risks . . . do things differently. Take on this sequence: change the conversation, have faith in your abilities, commit to leading your life, lock into a vision, find mentors and advisors, get direction, get help, and get going. Change is a great catalyst to increasing energy and shifting attitude. Stop doing what you've *been* doing if it's not working. Get in the sequence of success.

Freedom Day Is a Happy Day

You can, of course, choose to live small. It's easy; it's nice; not a lot of people will blame you—heck, they're doing it themselves. But what if your ancestors had done that? What if they'd stayed in the old country, in the village, on the farm, at the mill? What would your life be like now?

There are no rewards without risks. But really, how risky is it to lead your life and commit to creating something bigger and better for yourself and your family? Taking charge of your life and putting it in your own hands is actually the safest thing you can do. Who better than *you* to secure your future? Engage the Yes! Energy of extreme optimism and energy. The Equation will have you do less and make more of life.

CHAPTER 15

The Inquiry:

Are you comfortable with the norm, or motivated to move beyond it? What are you tolerating because "that's the way it has to be"? How often are you willing to go from no to yes, and to create change?

The Exercise:

1. Consider your current situation. Write down ways you could, using the *Energy Equation,* be less busy and more productive.

2. Examine each area of your life. If each could be the best it could be, what would that look like? Write or draw it in your journal.

3. Think about colleagues, peers, and friends who may want to get into a new conversation. Write down their names.

Next Steps:

Pick one specific part of your life that's not working that well, and change the conversation. Flip it so that it's positive.

Find some like-minded people and see if they want to engage in a new conversation.

List your gifts, and focus on one that can help you get into extreme optimism and energy.

1. What's the best team on which you've ever participated? What made it so appealing?

2. Whom could you team up with now to do less, make more?

3. List some mentors you'd like to model. Write down their contact information so you can follow through. These would be people you admire for the way they operate in business, in life, in their relationships, and/or with their friends and families.

4. What sequence of steps would work best for you in order to increase your energy and upshift your attitude into extreme optimism? Would building a team be an inspiring first step? Listing and focusing on your gifts? Taking time to find your core knowing and renewing your commitment to faith?

5. Fill in the factors for the *Energy Equation* in such a way that you can effect immediate change tomorrow:

$$\{\Delta C+ [F(2C)*D] +G+T\}S = \infty EOE\infty$$

ΔC—What is the conversation you're going to change?

F—How will this new experience fit with your faith?

2C—How can you draw upon your confidence and certainty?

D—How will this experience help you get closer to your dreams?

G—What gifts will you use?

T—Who will be on your team?

S—What will be your sequence of steps to take?

THE LEGACY OF YES!

One of the best things we can give young adults and children, whether our own or the ones in our lives, is confidence. Talent, intelligence, and even a good sense of humor will get you far, but confidence can take you all the way. A certainty, without arrogance, that comes from the calm knowing of a higher power and the ability to enroll others is a beautiful thing in adults *and* children.

As you move forward in Yes! Energy, it's important to share this new perspective and behavior with others. It's a powerful thing to reeducate those who are coming up in this world. If you believe that we need a more empowered, engaging, optimistic, energetic generation on our heels, then it is imperative that you teach the younger set to have Yes! Energy.

The *Energy Equation* should be part of your life every day. The younger people in your life—whether they are your children, grandchildren, nieces, nephews, students, clients, patients, or neighborhood and community friends—should see what it is you are doing to stay optimistic and solution oriented. By modeling you in your Yes! Energy, they will naturally incorporate extreme energy and optimism into their lives. Then they will have *that thing,* the "gift."

Begin by *changing the conversation.* Get rid of the old models, the scarcity language. Watch yourself when you tell kids that you or they can't afford something, or that a goal is too difficult. A helpful start is our program "Never Pay Your Kid An Allowance," available through the Loral Kids link at **http://www.liveoutloud .com**. Children provide a good arena in which to test your ability to change the conversation and pivot into more powerful language and ideas.

Talk about sourcing a higher power, and create the commitment to *faith*. It's never too early in life to learn that you are not the center of the universe. A child who understands the miracles of God and Spirit can appreciate levels of living that go beyond video games. Put, or at least suggest, time for spiritual exercise in children's schedules. Meditation is not only for adults. Most children don't have the opportunity to be fully in control of their lives. The idea that they can take a few minutes, every day, to connect with a core vibration, a source of knowing that they can call upon and to which they are accountable, can help them get into a solution orientation. This commitment also provides a huge foundation for *certainty* and *confidence*.

Most kids dream about what their future will be like. Encourage them to dream about what their best life can be like right now. Keep it realistic and doable, but push them to stretch beyond common expectations. This exercise will help young adults and children get into the swing of no-limit thinking, as well as challenge the rules of what's always been.

Everyone has gifts. Children have many, and childhood is prime time to uncover and nurture them. Encourage talents. Pay attention to skills you observe in kids that they might not value or appreciate, and promote them. Similarly, if a child reaches the point of frustration one too many times in a task or event, encourage him or her to enroll others to help. Building *team* at an early age is a good exercise in leadership. Teams can be displayed all over the place, be it at home or at school. The idea that community can be built and created in every facet of life, especially in environments children assume are competitive, will be refreshing, exciting, and comforting to them.

Finally, introduce young adults and children to *sequencing*. Do it in your own life so you can share with them your process and they can model it. Sequence your day with them; share what it is you're doing to visualize ahead of what you need to do. Then help them do the same.

Kids seem to have one project after another. This is a great way to introduce sequencing. We've all seen youngsters get overwhelmed by one task or another. The idea that they can take a moment to visualize and think ahead to what steps need to be taken and when is a wonderful tool. Sequencing can be applied to tasks, to daily schedules, to an overbooked evening of homework, to a weekend, a trip . . . anywhere, anytime. By learning to sequence now, children will have the ability to better approach and accomplish goals in the future.

It's time children understood that they, too, can actually have the Yes! Energy to do less, make more.

∞EOE∞

By sharing the *Energy Equation* with others, you will instill it in yourself.

It's time to build a life of optimism and energy for generations to come.

Begin now. Get into Yes! Energy and start living the best years of your life.

REFERENCES
& RESOURCES

Beckwith, Michael Bernard, *Spiritual Liberation: Fulfilling Your Soul's Potential*, Atria Books/Beyond Words, © 2009.

Bernstein, Peter L., *Against the Gods: The Remarkable Story of Risk*, Wiley, © 1998.

Brown, Les, *Live Your Dreams*, Harper Paperbacks, © 1994.

Canfield, Jack, *The Success Principles™: How to Get from Where You Are to Where You Want to Be*, HarperCollins, © 2006.

Chopra, Deepak, *The Seven Spiritual Laws of Success: A Practical Guide to the Fulfillment of Your Dreams*, New World Library/Amber-Allen Publishing, © 1994.

Clemons, Linda, **www.sisterpreneurinc.com**.

Collins, Jim, *Good to Great: Why Some Companies Make The Leap . . . and Others Don't*, Harper Business, © 2001

Collins, Jim, and Porras, Jerry, *Built to Last: Successful Habits of Visionary Companies*, Harper Business, © 1994.

Dyer, Wayne W., *Inspiration: Your Ultimate Calling*, Hay House, © 2007.

Goldratt, Eliyahu, and Cox, Jeff, *The Goal: A Process of Ongoing Improvement*, North River Press, © 2004.

Gray, John, *What You Feel, You Can Heal*, John Gray's Mars Venus LLC, © 1993.

Hanlon, Martha, and Williams, Chris, *Customers Are the Answer to Everything*, Morgan James Publishing, © 2012.

Hay, Louise L., *Love Yourself, Heal Your Life Workbook*, Hay House, © 1990.

————. *You Can Heal Your Life,* Hay House, © 1999.

Hill, Napoleon, *Think and Grow Rich: The Original Version, Restored and Revised,* Aventine Press, © 2004.

King, Martin Luther, Jr., "I Have A Dream" speech, delivered August 28, 1963.

Leonard, George, *Mastery: The Keys to Success and Long-Term Fulfillment,* Plume, © 1992.

Nichols, Lisa, *No Matter What!: 9 Steps to Living the Life You Love,* Wellness Central, © 2009.

Proctor, Bob, *You Were Born Rich,* Life Success Products, © 1997.

Tolle, Eckhart, *The Power of Now: A Guide to Spiritual Enlightenment,* Namaste Publishing/New World Library, © 1999.

Virtue, Doreen, *How to Hear Your Angels,* Hay House, © 2007.

Whitworth, Laura; Kinsey-House, Henry; and Sandahl, Phil, *Co-Active Coaching: New Skills for Coaching People Toward Success in Work and Life,* Davies-Black Publishing, © 1998.

Williamson, Marianne, *A Return to Love: Reflections on the Principles of A Course in Miracles,* Harper Paperbacks, © 1992.

ACKNOWLEDGMENTS

I am so very grateful for the gifts that come from God and to the amazing people who have been placed in my path. Thank you to all the people in my life: the engaging, energetic, and exciting team I get to serve; and those who serve me.

Thank you to Reid Tracy, president and CEO of Hay House, for your encouragement of, and support on, this endeavor. Thank you, too, to your great team, including Leon Nacson, Jill Kramer, Shannon Littrell, Rosie Barry, Gail Gonzales, Nancy Levin, Christy Salinas, and Alex Freemon. This type of book is new for me, but covers a topic that means a lot to me, and I appreciate the opportunity to share it through your first-class operation.

A big huge thank-you to Caroline Sherman for putting it all together. Thank you to the affiliates and joint-venture partners who contributed to, and directed the vision of, this book by telling us the concepts they'd like covered.

I continue to be grateful to the members of our Live Out Loud Community. What a great world we've created. Thank you to each and every member of Loral's Big Table and Loral's Big Table Alumni. You are changing the conversation to a Yes! conversation and using your gifts to make the world a better place. Thank you, too, to all those who attend Cash Machine/3 Days To Cash workshops and Live Out Loud seminars. That's where it all starts, by changing lives.

Thank you to the entire Live Out Loud staff, each of whom truly gives their all to be on this team. Thank you to the families who support those in our community so that they can give so much of themselves. Thanks to Martha Hanlon, Randy Tate, Nick Lawler, and Dona Donato for your specific ideas for this book. And to my Australian partner, Martyn Bell, his family, and now the Sydney team of mates . . . heaps of fun.

Thanks to my friends and dear confidants—you know who you are. To my family: I know you are always there. And thank you, most of all, to the best Yes! gifts ever given to me—my children, Logan and Tristin.

ABOUT THE AUTHOR

Loral Langemeier is one of today's most visible and innovative money experts. Because of her tenacity and absolute confidence in what she teaches, Langemeier is one of only a handful of women in the world today who can claim the title of "expert" when it comes to financial matters and the making of millionaires. She accelerates the conversation about money, sharing how to not just survive this tough economic climate, but how to succeed and thrive. She is the best-selling author of the *Millionaire Maker* series and *Put More Cash in Your Pocket,* as well as a leading entrepreneurial speaker and the CEO and founder of Live Out Loud, Inc., a multimillion-dollar company.

Websites: **www.yesenergybook.com, www.liveoutloud.com,** and **www.liveoutloudaustralia.com.au**

A Gift from Loral

Congratulations!

You now possess the basic formula to accomplish your goals, reach your dreams, do less and make more. By buying and reading this book, you have taken the first step to understanding your Yes! Energy and how it will change your life.

Now it's time to learn how to use it!

This book was just the beginning of your journey. I want to personally walk you through how to use the Yes! Energy formula to actively improve EVERY area of your life.

This is your exclusive invitation to access our FREE 8-Week Online Roadmap to Find Your Yes! Energy. You will receive valuable coaching that will show you, step-by-step, how to easily apply the Yes! Energy equation to your personal life.

Get ready to live with extreme optimism and energy every day. All you need to do is take action!

Go to FindYourYesEnergy.com and grab your gift.

NOTES

NOTES

NOTES

NOTES

NOTES

NOTES

NOTES

NOTES

NOTES

NOTES

NOTES

NOTES

NOTES

NOTES

Hay House Titles of Related Interest

YOU CAN HEAL YOUR LIFE, the movie,
starring Louise L. Hay & Friends
(available as a 1-DVD program and an expanded 2-DVD set)
Watch the trailer at: **www.LouiseHayMovie.com**

THE SHIFT, the movie,
starring Dr. Wayne W. Dyer
(available as a 1-DVD program and an expanded 2-DVD set)
Watch the trailer at: **www.DyerMovie.com**

∞

EUFEELING!: The Art of Creating Inner Peace and Outer Prosperity,
by Dr. Frank J. Kinslow (available July 2012)

THE FATIGUE SOLUTION: Increase Your Energy in Eight Easy Steps,
by Eva Cwynar, M.D., with Sharyn Kolberg

*THE MINDFUL MANIFESTO: How Doing Less and
Noticing More Can Help Us Thrive in a Stressed-Out World,*
by Dr. Jonty Heaversedge & Ed Halliwell

*MONEY, AND THE LAW OF ATTRACTION:
Learning to Attract Wealth, Health, and Happiness,*
by Esther and Jerry Hicks (The Teachings of Abraham®)

*WHO ARE YOU? A Success Process for Building
Your Life's Foundation,* by Stedman Graham

*THE WON THING: The "One" Secret to
a Totally Fulfilling Life,* by Peggy McColl

All of the above are available at your local bookstore,
or may be ordered by contacting Hay House (see next page).

∞

We hope you enjoyed this Hay House book.
If you'd like to receive our online catalog featuring
additional information on Hay House books and
products, or if you'd like to find out more about the
Hay Foundation, please contact:

Hay House, Inc., P.O. Box 5100, Carlsbad, CA 92018-5100
(760) 431-7695 or (800) 654-5126
(760) 431-6948 (fax) or (800) 650-5115 (fax)
www.hayhouse.com® • **www.hayfoundation.org**

∞

Published and distributed in Australia by:
Hay House Australia Pty. Ltd., 18/36 Ralph St., Alexandria NSW 2015
Phone: 612-9669-4299 • *Fax:* 612-9669-4144 • www.hayhouse.com.au

Published and distributed in the United Kingdom by:
Hay House UK, Ltd., 292B Kensal Rd., London W10 5BE
Phone: 44-20-8962-1230 • *Fax:* 44-20-8962-1239 • www.hayhouse.co.uk

Published and distributed in the Republic of South Africa by:
Hay House SA (Pty), Ltd., P.O. Box 990, Witkoppen 2068
Phone/Fax: 27-11-467-8904 • www.hayhouse.co.za

Published in India by: Hay House Publishers India,
Muskaan Complex, Plot No. 3, B-2, Vasant Kunj, New Delhi 110 070
Phone: 91-11-4176-1620 • *Fax:* 91-11-4176-1630 • www.hayhouse.co.in

Distributed in Canada by: Raincoast, 9050 Shaughnessy St.,
Vancouver, B.C. V6P 6E5 • *Phone:* (604) 323-7100
Fax: (604) 323-2600 • www.raincoast.com

∞

<u>Take Your Soul on a Vacation</u>

Visit **www.HealYourLife.com®** to regroup,
recharge, and reconnect with your own magnificence.
Featuring blogs, mind-body-spirit news, and
life-changing wisdom from Louise Hay and friends.

Visit **www.HealYourLife.com** today!